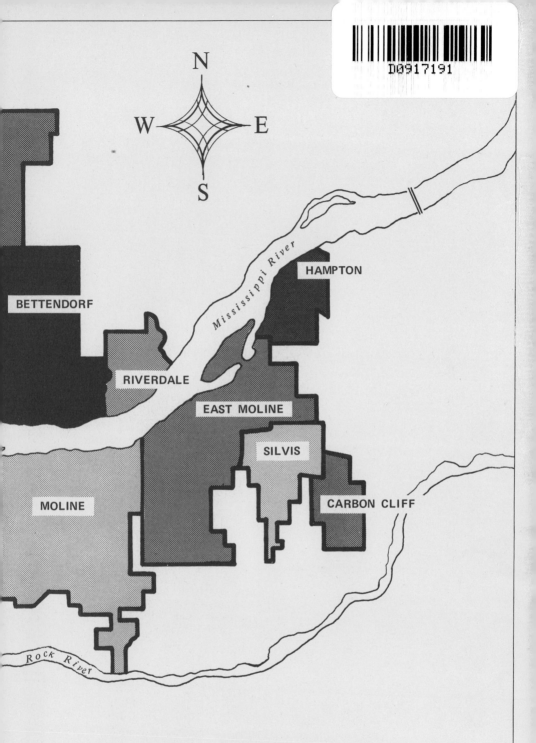

N
W • E
S

Mississippi River

HAMPTON

BETTENDORF

RIVERDALE

EAST MOLINE

SILVIS

MOLINE

CARBON CLIFF

Rock River

the greater QUAD-CITY area

METROPOLITAN

POLITICAL STRUCTURE

METROPOLITAN
POLITICAL STRUCTURE:

Intergovernmental Relations
and Political Integration
in the Quad-Cities

H. PAUL FRIESEMA

UNIVERSITY OF IOWA PRESS  IOWA CITY

Library of Congress Catalog Card Number: 73–147925
University of Iowa Press, Iowa City, Iowa 52240
© 1971 by The University of Iowa. All rights reserved
Printed in the United States of America
ISBN 87745–020–X

CONTENTS

TABLES

FOREWORD

Interjurisdictional activity within metropolitan areas has always seemed so complicated and uncoordinated that reform efforts, which would result in organizational simplification, have seemed desirable on that score alone. In this book Paul Friesema suggests that a large part of the metropolitan interjurisdictional "jungle" occurs because of scholarly and reform-induced myopia; not conditions in the metropolitan areas. Be that as it may, it certainly is surprising that more scholars have not addressed themselves to Mr. Friesema's fundamental question: how can we account for the remarkable staying power of metropolitan political systems composed of so many separate jurisdictions?

There are, to be sure, some rich theoretical arguments in the more recent literature on metropolitan politics—some of which are examined in this study, and some of which have appeared since the field work was completed. Yet no other work, to my knowledge, marshals such a wide range of empirical evidence.

As Mr. Friesema notes, this book is essentially a mapping exercise: a wide-ranging search for all of the different ways in which activities among separate jurisdictions become coordinated in this one metropolitan area. It seems likely that on the basis of this groundwork, it will be possible to construct, with some confidence, summary measures of coordination which ought to make the comparative study of metropolitan politics more fruitful.

While Paul Friesema's study is most valuable as a detailed empirical re-examination of some fundamental ideas about metropolitan politics, some intriguing suggestions come, where the data analysis is necessarily thin. Surely the suggestions which are advanced about the existence of a sense of metropolitan community not only in the Quad-Cities, but perhaps as a normal occurrence in American metropolitan areas, and the introductory exploration of the prospect for political integration even without contact between jurisdictions, deserve follow-up.

I am particularly impressed with the Quad-City political and governmental leaders—the respondents in this study. They seem to be a remarkably adaptive set of public officials, successfully overcoming barriers which have perplexed many of their ivory tower observers. But the barriers remain. Metropolitan reform may still be "righteous," as Robert Wood once labeled the reform impulse. Even righteous reformers will benefit from a perspective in which they view unification as an *alternate* order, rather than as order in place of chaos.

DEAN ZENOR

1971

ACKNOWLEDGMENTS

Acknowledgments are due to an uncommonly large number of friends who have materially assisted this study. Professor Samuel C. Patterson of The University of Iowa has given me considerable assistance and encouragement in the study, even though the subject was outside his own academic area of interest. I thank him for his tolerance. Professor Deil Wright, now of the University of North Carolina, has provided valuable help at many stages in this undertaking. Professor Scott Greer of Northwestern has opened doors, intellectual and otherwise, for which I am most grateful.

Dr. Dean Zenor, Director of the Institute of Public Affairs at The University of Iowa, has provided valuable counsel as this study has progressed. I hope the product of this study will help repay the debt I owe the Institute of Public Affairs for the time and assistance made available to me. The help provided by my close friends and colleagues at the Institute is most gratefully acknowledged. David Paulsmeyer, as my associate during the early stages of this project, provided help far beyond the call of his interviewing duties. His programming assistance was substantial.

My wife Jane has been patient and helpful during this long research endeavor. She has also provided methodological help at some key points in the project.

Finally, the many Quad-City area public officials and other informants were almost uniformly helpful and tolerant, although some must have felt that the questions asked of them were naive or unimportant. The mayors were especially helpful. I appreciate what they provided me.

1

The Study of Political

Integration in Metropolitan Areas

This book is a study of metropolitan political structure. It explores patterns of intergovernmental activity and other processes of political integration which occur among municipal governments in the Quad-City metropolitan area of Illinois and Iowa. This metropolitan area, despite its common name, is composed of the five industrial cities of Davenport, Iowa; Rock Island, Illinois; Moline, Illinois; East Moline, Illinois; and Bettendorf, Iowa, plus smaller municipalities. The metropolitan area is bisected by the Mississippi River, which is also the state boundary. This study attempts to analyze why and how the separate jurisdictions within the area can continue to operate and deal with metropolitan political issues.

The first chapter discusses current interpretations about metropolitan political structure and the processes of political integration of metropolitan areas. It also discusses the general approach of the study, some problems encountered by the use of this approach, and concludes with a discussion of the multinuclear and interstate character of the Quad-City metropolitan area, with emphasis on how these conditions affect the study. Chapter 2 develops the historical patterns of integration in the Quad-City area, discusses the existence of a sense of metropolitan community, and ends with a brief description of municipal government organization in the area. Subsequent chapters present and analyze a number of transaction measures and other integrative indicators gathered for the study. These measures were meant to cover as exhaustive a range of potential integrative processes as possible. The patterns of interjurisdictional competition and specialization within the Quad-City area are also examined, and the study concludes with an analysis of interjurisdictional conflict and its impact upon the political structure of the metropolitan community.

INTERGOVERNMENTAL RELATIONS AND THE POLITICAL INTEGRATION OF METROPOLITAN AREAS[1]

American metropolitan areas are composed of many formally autonomous political units located in very close proximity to one another. This has been the pattern of political organization for virtually all American metropolitan areas during most of the twentieth century. Despite the stability of this pattern of political organization, and voluminous literature analyzing metropolitan political problems, it remains unclear how and to what extent the separate jurisdictions within metropolitan areas actually deal with one another.

The lack of analysis of relationships among jurisdictions within metropolitan areas probably can be traced to the reform tradition of metropolitan government research. Many reform-minded political scientists have been concerned about the problems of disorganized and fractionated governmental structure of American metropolitan areas for a long time.[2] These problems have seemed so clear that efforts to measure systematic relationships between jurisdictions have rarely been carried out. The resolution of the metropolitan problem has appeared obvious. Some form of unification of governments into a single jurisdiction has seemed necessary.[3] Reform literature is barren of explanations for the remarkable successes of the metropolitan areas in building transportation networks, avoiding unacceptable spillover effects from one jurisdiction's actions to another, achieving non-conflicting land use patterns, and otherwise surviving in this pattern of multiple governments.

In the middle 1950s a new focus entered the literature on metropolitan political structure. A more systematic effort to explore the metropolitan community became apparent. Charles Adrian identified this work as the

1. Some of this material is drawn from my article, "The Metropolis and the Maze of Local Government," *Urban Affairs Quarterly* 2 (December 1966), 68–90.
2. Paul Studenski wrote *Government of Metropolitan Areas* (New York: National Municipal League) in 1930. For the next twenty-five years political scientists basically accepted and reiterated the Studenski analysis, often losing some of his remarkable insights along the way.
3. For a digest of metropolitan surveys and studies see Governmental Affairs Foundation, *Metropolitan Surveys: A Digest* (Chicago: Public Administration Service, 1958). Some critical analyses of this relatively sterile literature are found in Lawrence J. R. Herson, "The Lost World of Municipal Government," *American Political Science Review* 51 (June 1957), 330–345; Wallace S. Sayre and Nelson W. Polsby, "American Political Science and the Study of Urbanization," in Philip M. Hauser and Leo F. Schnore, eds., *The Study of Urbanization* (New York: John Wiley & Sons, 1965); Robert O. Warren, *Government in Metropolitan Regions: A Reappraisal of Fractionated Political Organization* (Davis: Institute of Governmental Affairs, University of California, 1966).

product of a "second generation" of metropolitan researchers.[4] The most noteworthy element in this newer tradition has been a commitment to rigorous empirical research upon the politics and government of metropolitan areas. These new metropolitan researchers have characteristically not eschewed policy positions; their commitment to reform has been about as strong as their predecessors'. This newer tradition has produced an immense volume of literature which has incrementally improved understanding of the metropolis, and has not simply applied general "truths" to one more metropolitan area. Such newer orientation toward metropolitan research has about carried the field. Municipal officials' professional journals reflect this orientation, and many of the principal researchers are travelers on the "municipal problems" and "urban affairs" banquet circuit. Federal agencies, particularly the Advisory Commission on Intergovernmental Relations, also reflect this new approach. A new standard interpretation of the field has been established, many findings having achieved the status of "conventional wisdom," no longer in need of footnote citation.

Some of the major academic figures who have created this new tradition are Robert Wood, Roscoe Martin, Winston Crouch, John C. Bollens, Henry J. Schmandt, Scott Greer, Frank Smallwood, Edward Sofen, David A. Booth,[5] and others. This is quite a mixed group of scholars and they do not constitute a self-conscious "school" of thought, beyond a common interest in metropolitan political organization. They do share a commit-

4. Charles Adrian, "Metropology: Folklore and Field Research," *Public Administration Review* 21 (Summer 1961), 153.
5. Robert C. Wood, *1400 Governments* (Garden City: Doubleday and Co., Anchor Books, 1961); *Suburbia: Its People and Their Politics* (Boston: Houghton-Mifflin Co., 1958). Roscoe C. Martin, *Metropolis in Transition: Local Government Adaptation to Changing Urban Needs* (Washington, D.C.: H.H.F.A., 1963); _____ et al., *Decisions in Syracuse* (Bloomington: Indiana University Press, 1961); _____ and Douglas Price, *The Metropolis and Its Problems* (Syracuse: Syracuse University Seminar on Metropolitan Research, 1959). Winston Crouch and Beatrice Dinerman, *Southern California Metropolis: A Study in Development of Government for a Metropolitan Area* (Berkeley and Los Angeles: University of California Press, 1964); Winston Crouch, *Intergovernmental Relations*, Metropolitan Los Angeles Study, vol. 15 (Los Angeles: Haynes Foundation, 1954). John C. Bollens, ed., *Exploring the Metropolitan Community* (Berkeley and Los Angeles: University of California Press, 1961); _____ and Henry Schmandt, *The Metropolis: Its People, Politics and Economic Life* (New York: Harper & Row, 1965). Henry Schmandt and William H. Standing, *The Milwaukee Metropolitan Study Commission* (Bloomington: Indiana University Press, 1965). Scott Greer, *The Emerging City: Myth and Reality* (New York: Free Press of Glencoe, 1962); *Governing the Metropolis* (New York: John Wiley & Sons, 1962); *Metropolitics: A Study of Political Culture* (New York: John Wiley & Sons, 1963). Frank Smallwood, *Greater London: The Politics of Metropolitan Reform* (Indianapolis: Bobbs-Merrill Co., 1965). Edward Sofen, *The Miami Metropolitan Experiment* (Bloomington: Indiana University Press, 1963). David A. Booth, *Metropolitics: The Nashville Consolidation* (East Lansing: Institute for Community Development and Service, Michigan State University, 1963).

ment to empirical research upon metropolitan questions, a sympathy with and often a direct connection to the reform movement, and perhaps a common pessimism about its prospects.

Scholars in the new tradition also share certain interpretations about metropolitan political organization. As distinguished from the previous reform tradition, these researchers consider relationships between jurisdictions. They do not ignore the question, assuming relationships to be nonexistent. Many writers in this new tradition assert that intergovernmental relations between local jurisdictions in metropolitan areas are sporadic, and on an ad hoc basis.[6] A consistent corollary is that is is partially the inability or unwillingness of the jurisdictions within metropolitan areas to resolve issues and jointly provide services on a sustained basis that creates the "problem" of metropolitan areas.

The term ad hoc is a relatively imprecise concept, but it is used as a conventional description of relations between jurisdictions in metropolitan areas. The dictionary defines ad hoc to mean "for this case alone: special," but it is quite difficult to see what the metropolitan researchers would consider as non ad hoc relationships. Presumably non ad hoc relationships would be recurring and in some way systematic political activity. Metropolitan researchers use the term ad hoc to describe two different but related aspects of relationships within metropolitan areas. The first use concerns *administrative* transactions between governments in which it is thought that there is a lack of relationship or pattern from one transaction to another, and each transaction is conceived to be struck anew with each issue which arises.[7] An example would be an exchange of information about a car theft between police in different jurisdictions, entirely unrelated to other relationships which might occur between the departments or jurisdictions. The second meaning is more concerned with *political decision-making*.[8] In this usage each problem or event requiring a metropolitan or interjurisdictional decision is perceived as being handled through a decision-making process which is *sui generis*, with problems independently treated, without relation, one to another. Thus there would be no pattern of accommodation, no

---

6. See, for example, Bollens and Schmandt, The Metropolis, p. 180; Crouch, "Conflict and Cooperation Among Local Governments in the Metropolis," Annals 359 (May 1965), 67; Greer, The Emerging City, p. 199; Martin et al., Decisions in Syracuse, p. 337; Wallace Sayre and Herbert Kaufman, Governing New York City (New York: Russell Sage Foundation, 1961), p. 594; Wood, "A Division of Power in Metropolitan Areas" in Arthur Maass, ed., Area and Power (New York: Free Press of Glencoe, 1959), p. 66.
7. This seems to be the meaning in Crouch, "Conflict and Cooperation Among Local Governments in the Metropolis," 67; Sayre and Kaufman, Governing New York City, p. 594.
8. For this use see, for example, Bollens and Schmandt, The Metropolis; Greer, The Emerging City, p. 199.

system of deference to other actors, nor any other regularized structure for achieving agreement between the jurisdictions. While these two uses of *ad hoc* are distinct, they are sometimes used interchangeably.[9] They do have common elements, in that with either use relations between jurisdictions are sporadic and unsystematic. Each issue which arises must be resolved without benefit of precedence or pattern.

The evidence to support either meaning of *ad hoc* is less than persuasive. The few reported measures of *administrative* transactions lead to a different conclusion.[10] From these reports transactions between officials in metropolitan areas seem to be frequent and patterned, and, in fact, many relationships are written into state law. Unless public officials ignore mandatory legal requirements, and do not take advantage of beneficial permissive legislation, many relationships are surely not *ad hoc* in the administrative sense. Even contractual agreements between jurisdictions, sometimes cited as evidence of *ad hoc* cooperation, almost always last for years. This necessarily means that in implementing such contracts, relationships are enduring and systematic. The *political decision-making* interpretation also raises some questions. The primary method used to derive this description of the *ad hoc* decision-making process has been the case study, which is surely an inappropriate way to uncover non *ad hoc* relationships which may exist. Case studies focus upon major events, over a narrow time span, and any pattern between decisions examined in the case and other decisions remains unrecorded. Contacts between decision-makers over other issues are undisclosed. Thus the evidence that interjurisdictional relationships are *ad hoc* is not convincing, and obscures important interpretive questions.[11] A related characterization of local intergovernmental relations deserves examination. Scholars tend to assert or assume that such contact as occurs between jurisdictions is based on *quid pro quo* arrangements, occurring under conflict conditions and involving hard bargaining. But the case studies, focusing upon major controversial issues, and avoiding standard, preprogrammed, or repetitious decisions, may distort events in the real metropolitan world. For if relations between jurisdictions are frequent and stable, it seems likely that other accommodations have been worked out. In fact, it is not clear whether frequent relations *could* even be *quid pro*

9. See Martin et al., *Decisions in Syracuse*, p. 337.
10. Thomas R. Dye et al., "Differentiation and Cooperation in a Metropolitan Area," *Midwest Journal of Political Science* 7 (May 1962), 145–155; W. Brooke Graves, "Interlocal Relations," in *American Intergovernmental Relations* (New York: Charles Scribner's Sons, 1964), pp. 737–779; H. Paul Friesema, *Communications, Coordination and Control Among Local Governments in the Siouxland: A Study of Intergovernmental Relations* (Iowa City: Institute of Public Affairs, University of Iowa, 1965).
11. Some of the best of these case studies are found in Edward Banfield, *Political Influence* (New York: Free Press of Glencoe, 1961); Martin et al., *Decisions in Syracuse*; Robert Mowitz and Deil S. Wright, *Profile of a Metropolis* (Detroit: Wayne State University Press, 1962).

quo. How, for example, could interpersonal advice and consultations be *quid pro quo* if one jurisdiction is superior in technical or professional skill? How could joint or mutual service agreements be *quid pro quo*, between jurisdictions with vastly different resources? These are important, but unexamined questions, if we wish to understand the operations of metropolitan political systems.

No clear picture or theory emerges from this research to explain how the jurisdictions are able to continue operating effectively (or at all). While scholars in the new tradition of metropolitan research discuss interjurisdictional activity, and usually claim it is inadequate to the problems of the metropolis, they do not provide much guidance as to what maintains the system. The closest to a theory of metropolitan political integration that can be derived from this research is that problems of metropolitan or interjurisdictional importance are resolved or patched up only as they reach some critical threshold, and then are only minimally resolved, often resulting in just postponing the date of some inevitable denouement.

A few scholars concerned with metropolitan political organization do not adopt the orientation or, in most cases, the policy preferences of this "second generation" tradition of metropolitan research. Some of them have been developing other theoretical orientations which contribute to understanding the processes presently maintaining metropolitan political systems.[12] Some have proposed that the continued existence and strength of metropolitan systems may be explained best by the operation of natural or unconscious forces in the metropolis, under some variant of a "mutual adjustment" process.[13] The force they see at work is characteristically listed as some kind of market mechanism, which provides for the intelligent sorting out of people and governments throughout the metropolitan terrain. With this distribution system in play, it is argued, the jurisdictions can

12. I have benefited from reading Henry J. Schmandt's unpublished background paper "Toward Comparability in Metropolitan Research." It was prepared for the conference on Comparative Research in Community Politics held at the University of Georgia, November 16–19, 1966. The order which I impose upon the disparate research discussed below is somewhat different, but quite compatible with Schmandt's ordering of these studies.

13. The theory of mutual adjustment is most rigorously presented in Charles E. Lindblom, *The Intelligence of Democracy: Decision Making Through Mutual Adjustment* (New York: Free Press of Glencoe, 1965). Some of the major exponents of a theory of this kind with regard to metropolitan political organization are, in addition to Lindblom, Vincent Ostrom et al., "The Organization of Government in Metropolitan Areas: A Theoretical Inquiry," *American Political Science Review* 55 (December 1961), 831–834; Edward Banfield and Morton Grodzins, *Government and Housing in Metropolitan Areas* (New York: McGraw-Hill, 1958).

While I have listed Winston Crouch among the "second generation" or new tradition metropolitan researchers, the book of Crouch and Dinerman, *Southern California Metropolis*, has a theory of "countervailing forces" that is also a variation on the mutual adjustment theme.

continue to operate as relatively independent units, without debilitating conflict, and without the necessity of direct coordination through bargaining or some form of hierarchical structure.

Vincent Ostrom, and his associates, in particular, also stress that direct relations between jurisdictions are frequent, systematic, and well-entrenched. But this is not the thrust of their essential theoretical argument.[14] They argue that metropolitan systems are maintained because the market separates people into groups of municipal-service-receiving local citizens, who do not demand or require services provided on a different basis than they are receiving them. The Lindblom thesis stresses a different aspect of "mutual adjustment." In its metropolitan form, the argument is that a good deal of coordinated activity occurs without direct contact between jurisdictions because the jurisdictions constantly take account of each other in their own decision-making. Even without direct contact or agreement, one city, for example, in making its plans, includes intelligence about what the other cities are doing or have done. Lindblom persuasively argues that this provides a major explanation of order maintenance which has been almost overlooked by social scientists who have insisted upon a need for some kind of direct coordination of activity. Metropolitan studies, it seems, will have to consider, at least residually, the integration of political activity in metropolitan areas which occurs without the need for direct coordination or contact.[15]

Another important approach to understanding metropolitan political organization is to treat metropolitan systems as analogous to international systems, and to apply theoretical models developed for studying international politics to the metropolitan arena. Two attempts to make such an analogy are particularly important antecedents to this study. These contributions are by Matthew Holden, Jr., and by Karl W. Deutsch and others using Deutsch's analytic framework.[16] Professor Holden posits three characteristics of what he labels "diplomatic systems," as being important in both the international and the metropolitan arena.

14. Vincent Ostrom et al., "Organization of Government in Metropolitan Areas"; Robert Warren, "Political Form and Metropolitan Reform," *Public Administration Review* 24 (September 1964), 180–187.
15. To date much of the commentary on these theoretical approaches has been to criticize the tendency of these scholars to equate what is with what ought to be. The argument is that because these scholars find that a system does exist and persist, therefore, they believe that it is valuable and ought to be retained. I believe the criticism of this conservative bias is valid, especially as applied to Ostrom, Warren et al., and Banfield. On the other hand, the critics have no basis on this ground to reject or ignore what "is."
16. Matthew Holden, Jr., "The Governance of the Metropolis as a Problem in Diplomacy," *Journal of Politics* 26 (August 1964), 627–647. Philip Jacob and James Toscano, eds., *The Integration of Political Communities* (Philadelphia and New York: J. B. Lippincott, 1964).

1. Diplomatic systems are social systems consisting of corporate units bound within an 'ecological community.' These corporate units are the *primary* actors in the system. . . .
2. Diploma'tic systems are not political communities in that they lack a sufficiently thorough *symbol* system, an adequate *deliberative* process for arriving at system decisions, and an adequate *administrative* process for assuring reasonable execution of such decisions as might be reached. . . .
3. Diplomatic communication is governed by a ritual which proscribes nongovernmental initiatives toward the resolution of substantive issues in which governments are partisans. [All italics are Holden's.]

While Holden's characterizations will not be accepted *a priori*, the categories of data which he derivatively asserts should be gathered are most useful. He suggests essentially that it will be necessary to gather information upon the direct interactions between component units in metropolitan areas. He asserts the need for systematic data upon the subject matter of interactions; the relative status and power of the actor-governments involved in interaction; the permanence and transcience of interaction (and especially the question of the legacy of conflict); and the procedures of interaction. Holden regards these categories as the fundamental political framework of the metropolis.

> At any particular time, these will set the outer limits beyond which manipulation is not feasible. Within these limits, however, manipulation is a function of the procedures of interaction or methods of doing business deliberately. The three sub-aspects which seem open to inquiry are: (1) frequency and instrumentalities of interaction, (2) scope of interaction, and (3) forms of ultimate conflict.[17]

In discussing the forms of "ultimate conflict" in metropolitan areas, Holden conceives of litigation as the functional equivalent to war in the international system.[18]

17. Holden, "Governance of the Metropolis," 633.
18. Holden, "Governance of the Metropolis," 635. One difficulty with this suggestive analogy is that the resolution of "ultimate conflict" in the metropolitan arena may not be based upon any calculus of relative power of the litigants, at least as power is conceived in international relations. A small, resource-poor, neighboring jurisdiction to a municipal giant, under normal circumstances may win a bilateral legal dispute with the giant (or it may not). One cannot conceive of Haiti besting the United States in a bilateral war, under normal circumstances. This means that there is a much larger element of unpredictability in the resolution of metropolitan ultimate conflict as compared to what there is in the international system. In turn, the value of an implicit threat of resorting to "ultimate conflict" is quite different in normal negotiations within the two types of systems. For an entirely different hypothesis concerning the role of litigation in metropolitan conflict resolution see Friesema, *Communications, Coordination and Control Among Local Governments in the Siouxland: A Study of Intergovernmental Relations*, 36.

All of the suggestions for categorizing information about metropolitan polities are relevant to this study, which will present data on many of these very points.

The book edited by Jacob and Toscano, *The Integration of Political Communities*, represents a major experimental attempt to apply Karl Deutsch's work on the political integration of nations and transnational areas to the study of metropolitan areas.[19] Deutsch's theory of political integration, as developed in his work on nations and internation areas, is very complex. The major concepts that he has developed, which seem to have applicability in studying metropolitan political integration are summarized by Holden:

Security-community: a group of people which has become integrated.

Integration: attainment, within a territory, of a 'sense of community' and of institutions and practices strong enough and widespread enough to assure for a 'long' time dependable expectations of 'peaceful change' among its population.

Sense of Community: belief on the part of individuals within a group that they have come to agreement on at least this one point—that common social problems must and can be resolved by processes of 'peaceful change.'

Peaceful Change: resolution of social problems, normally by institutionalized procedures without resort to large-scale physical force.

'Pluralistic' security-communities are those in which there is integration but no common government.

19. Deutsch's work on international and national integration is found in many sources. Some of the major works are Karl W. Deutsch, *Nationalism and Social Communication: An Inquiry into the Foundations of Nationalism* (Cambridge: M.I.T. Press, 1953); *Political Community at the International Level* (Garden City, N.Y.: Doubleday & Co., 1954); Karl W. Deutsch et al., *Political Community and the North Atlantic Area* (Princeton: Princeton University Press, 1957). Professor Deutsch has developed a communications theory of political behavior in *The Nerves of Government: Models of Political Communication and Control* (New York: Free Press of Glencoe, 1963).

The Jacob and Toscano book is not the only attempt to apply either Deutsch's theory of political integration or a communications model to the study of urban and metropolitan areas. Louis H. Masotti has independently applied Deutsch's concept of integration in his dissertation "The Politics of Plural Communities: The Process of Political Integration in a Multi-Municipality High School District" (Ph.D. diss. Northwestern University, 1964). See also the Holden article cited above. There have been other attempts to apply a "communications approach" for urban studies not based upon Deutsch's international integration work, but rather upon the development of cybernetic models of political and social phenomena which Deutsch has championed. See Richard L. Meier, *A Communications Theory of Urban Growth* (Cambridge: M.I.T. Press, 1962); Seymour J. Mandelbaum, *Boss Tweed's New York* (New York: John Wiley & Sons, 1965); Friesema, *Communications, Coordination and Control Among Local Governments in the Siouxland: A Study of Intergovernmental Relations.*

'Amalgamated' security-communities are those in which there are common governments.[20]

These concepts seem readily transferable to the study of metropolitan political integration.

Most analyses using this framework assume or assert that no security community exists for metropolitan areas. Thus, much of the discussion concerns what would be the necessary conditions to create a metropolitan security community. Three background conditions are seen as particularly crucial in the development of an integrated "pluralistic" metropolitan community: the main politically relevant values of the participating units must be compatible; participating units must have the capability of responsive action; and the partners must be able to predict each other's behavior within an atmosphere of trust.[21] One other factor is also crucial, and that is the development of a metropolitan-wide leadership, transcending the jurisdictional lines. Professor Masotti, for example, writes:

> Within the political structure of the plural community, we submit that one factor above all others makes for integration in an important way—the evolution of a community-wide, supraunit leadership structure dedicated to the proposition that the plural community serves an important function and must be made effective.[22]

Professor Deutsch also asserts the need for operational indices of political integration. He discusses many cybernetically derived transaction measures which may be used as evidence of cohesion.[23] Many of these seem gatherable within metropolitan areas. While Deutsch suggests many transaction indicators, the ones developed in The Integration of Political Communities are personal mobility measures and interjurisdictional agreements.[24] When

20. Holden, "Governance of the Metropolis," 643. These concepts are quoted from Deutsch et al., Political Community and the North Atlantic Area. Deutsch has given slightly different, but compatible definitions of some of these concepts elsewhere.
21. Holden, "Governance of the Metropolis," 643–645; Masotti, "Politics of Plural Communities," p. 172.
22. Masotti, "Politics of Plural Communities," p. 12.
23. Karl W. Deutsch, "Transaction Flows as Indicators of Political Cohesion," in Jacob and Toscano, eds., The Integration of Political Communities. Deutsch has developed this argument, at different levels of technicality, in many places. See particularly Nationalism and Social Communication; I. Richard Savage and Karl W. Deutsch, "A Statistical Model of the Gross Analyses of Transaction Flows," Econometrica 28 (July 1960), 551–572. For one application of this approach to the historical study of Anglo-American community, see Bruce M. Russett, Community and Contention: Britain and America in the Twentieth Century (Cambridge: M.I.T. Press, 1963).
24. James V. Toscano, "Transaction Flow Analyses in Metropolitan Areas: Some Preliminary Explorations" in Jacob and Toscano, eds., The Integration of Political Communities, 98–119.

these suggestions are used, along with some from Holden and the "mutual adjustment" advocates, it becomes possible to study the persistence of the metropolitan form with a methodological approach that, at least in its potential, promises to improve knowledge of the operation of the metropolis.

PURPOSE OF QUAD-CITY STUDY

This study examines intergovernmental activity and other integrative aspects of political activity in the Quad-City area of Illinois and Iowa, and focuses upon activities within ten contiguous municipalities of the area. A political community exists among these municipalities which crowd together which is akin to what Deutsch conceptualizes as a pluralistic security-community. While no common local government exists, there is a "sense of community," and institutions and practices have been adopted to meet the needs of the citizens. It is expected that this system will continue to peacefully evolve, although federal compulsion may be speeding up the process of change. Thus this system meets Deutsch's criteria for a security-community. The simple and irrefutible fact that the separate governments continue to operate without significant breakdowns is sufficient evidence that a minimum degree of political integration has been achieved among these separate cities. The essential goal of this study is to delineate the processes by which this political integration is achieved.

The transaction measures of political integration which Deutsch and his associates describe are usually treated as *representative indicators* of political integration or cohesion, potentially interchangeable with other measures which could be gathered. While this study gathers many of the transaction measures suggested by Deutsch and his colleagues, its main purpose is somewhat different. This difference is important to note and explain. In this analysis we begin by positing that a plural political community exists in the Quad-Cities, and the research problem is to account for its maintenance. Thus the task is not to gather *representative indicators* of political integration, but to uncover and analyze the widest possible range of *processes* by which this integration is achieved and the Quad-City political community is maintained. An effort has been made to be as exhaustive and inclusive as possible, but inevitably the study falls short of its goal. Some potential processes of integration only came to attention while gathering data, too late for any systematic inclusion within the interviews. Perhaps, other means by which integration is achieved have just not been discovered.

The definition of the boundaries of the Quad-City community has arbitrarily been set as the borders of the ten contiguous municipalities of the

Quad-Cities. The area undoubtedly constitutes a "natural system" of inter-action in many ways. It seems to be true, for example, that many economic and social transactions flow freely throughout the ten municipality area, but drop off by some step level outside of its boundaries. On the other hand, the flow of political transactions within the area is not clear a priori.[25] For some activities the "natural" boundary, as determined by transaction flows, would surely be different than the ten municipalities' borders. There are some sixty-five cities, towns and villages in the three county area which constitutes the Davenport–Rock Island–Moline Standard Metropolitan Statistical Area. Even the exact boundaries of commitment to the "security-community" are not clear. Few residents would exclude any of the five major cities—the core of the community—from the Quad-City area (Davenport, Rock Island, Moline, East Moline, Bettendorf). But agreement as to which other municipalities are included within the Quad-City area varied from respondent to respondent. (Very few respondents defined their own municipality as outside the Quad-City area, whatever else they included within the area). Moreover, many other political units are involved in political activity which occurs within the geographic bounds of the ten municipalities. The Scott and Rock Island County governments, the school districts, the two state governments and the federal government are all deeply enmeshed in local political affairs.[26] But for purposes of this study these units will be defined as outside the system to be analyzed. Using David Easton's distinction between "natural systems" and analytic or "constructive" systems, the Quad-City area, as defined in this study, is an analytic or constructive system.[27]

With the Quad-City area defined as a pluralistic security community and

25. It is frequently asserted that economic and social transactions flow freely throughout metropolitan areas, without being affected by the city limits signs. On the other hand, political transactions are often purported to be confined, or largely so, within municipal borders. See Greer, The Emerging City: Myth and Reality, p. 175; Schmandt and Bollens, The Metropolis: Its People, Politics and Economic Life, p. 497; Amos H. Hawley and Basil G. Zimmer, "Resistance to Unification in a Metropolitan Community," in Morris Janowitz, ed., Community Political Systems (New York: Free Press of Glencoe, 1961), p. 148. I have challenged the adequacy of these assertions in the article "The Metropolis and the Maze of Local Government," Urban Affairs Quarterly 2 (December 1966), 78–80.
26. For a most enlightening discussion of the intertwined roles of all these types of governments at the local level see Morton Grodzins, The American System, ed. Daniel J. Elazar (Chicago: Rand, McNally & Co., 1966). See particularly Chapter 6, "The Bundle of Governmental Services," (156–189) in which Grodzins points out the ubiquitous nature of so-called "special relationships" to the federal government, which rationalize the federal government's role as a key local decision-making unit. The "special relationship" in the Quad-Cities is based upon the Rock Island Arsenal, the Corps of Engineers regional offices, and other federal activities on the Mississippi River.
27. David Easton, A Framework for Political Analysis (Englewood Cliffs, N.J.: Prentice-Hall, 1965).

as a political system composed of ten major subsystems, the next problem is to specify the particular transaction measures and other integrative measures gathered and analyzed in studying the processes by which this plural community is maintained. Until recently it has not been clear what transaction measures might be usefully gathered to study intergovernmental activities of local jurisdictions. Students of intergovernmental relations have had one ideal unit of measurement for the study of federal-state, state-local, and federal-local activity in financial transfers. Money is cardinal data, and information on financial transactions is often available in accessible form. Money transfers may also be of use in studying intra-metropolitan relations, but it seems clear that financial transfers do not account for much metropolitan activity.[28] Professor Deutsch's work suggests other transaction measures which seem more useful in dealing with metropolitan structure. One, already applied elsewhere, is to treat interjurisdictional agreements as a measure of cohesion,[29] and is the first process of integration analyzed in the Quad-City study.

Some students of intergovernmental relations have insisted that the key emphasis in the study of this field should be on interpersonal relations between governmental officials. William Anderson, for example, writes:

Intergovernmental relations are carried out through the actions of public governing bodies and governmental officials. . . . The concept of intergovernmental relations necessarily has to be formulated largely in terms of human relations and human behavior. . . .[30]

Deil S. Wright has gone even further:

Strictly speaking . . . there are no inter-governmental relations, there are only relations among officials who govern different units!

Relations are not a sometime thing, formally ratified in cooperative agreements or rigidly set by statutes and/or courts. Rather, the emphasis and concern of intergovernmental relations looks to the continuous, day-to-day,

28. For a broader discussion, see my *Communication, Coordination and Control Among Local Governments in the Siouxland: A Study of Intergovernmental Relations*, 1–2. An excellent example of how financial transactions can be the basis for sophisticated analysis of interlocal relations is found in Deil S. Wright and Edwin M. Van Bruggan, "Schools Versus Sewers: An Empirical Test of the Tax Competition Thesis" (Iowa City: Institute of Public Affairs, University of Iowa, 1966).
29. James V. Toscano, "Transaction Flow Analyses in Metropolitan Areas: Some Preliminary Explorations" in Jacob and Toscano, eds., *The Integration of Political Communities*, pp. 98–119. For other research on interjurisdictional agreements, see Chapter 3.
30. William Anderson, *Intergovernmental Relations in Review* (Minneapolis: University of Minnesota Press, 1960), p. 4.

patterns of contacts, knowledge, and evaluations of the officials who govern.[31]

Thus it is useful to consider transactions among public officials in the Quad-Cities as a major indicator of the processes of integration. All of the rest of the *direct* transaction measures will be of interpersonal relations between officials of the different jurisdictions.

The direct measures of intergovernmental personal communication which are useful in understanding integration are first the face-to-face meetings, telephone calls, and mail correspondence which occur in the course of work of public officials. For this study all such face-to-face, telephone and mail contacts are grouped together under the label "Direct Contact in the Course of Work." This listing almost exhausts the ways in which the public officials can directly have contact with one another in the course of work. The one additional type of direct interchange coded in this category is interpersonal radio contact. This was a method of exchange used by some police respondents, but no other public officials.

In addition to communication which occurs in the course of work, other direct interaction may occur among public officials, and may also be processes by which political activity is integrated.

One type of interpersonal transaction often identified with the integration of political activity is contact between public officials through municipal or professional associations.[32] Such communication is studied here as a second direct interpersonal channel for integrating political activity. Another potential channel for personal exchanges among public officials is through clubs and social, fraternal, or veterans organizations (many of them organized on an area-wide basis), which may provide a setting in which political activity between and among the separate jurisdictions is channeled. While some claim that political parties do not play much of a role in integrating activity between local governments, other studies provide illustrations of a contrary situation.[33] In this study of the Quad-City area it will be possible to measure political parties as forums of exchange between the governments and governmental officials. Business activities are also a potential source of interpersonal exchange. Many elected officials and some appointed ones are not engaged in public office on a full-time

31. Deil S. Wright, "Intergovernmental Relations and Environmental Change: What Role for the States." (Paper delivered at seminar on Political Dynamics of Environmental Change, Indiana University, Bloomington, March 18–20, 1965.)
32. Crouch, *Intergovernmental Relations*, p. 107; Grodzins, *The American System*, p. 71; Ira Sharkansky, "Intergovernmental Relations in Brevard County, Florida: An Exploratory Study" (Urban Research Center, Florida State University, 1966), p. 19.
33. Some case studies which suggest that, at least upon occasion, parties may serve to integrate activity between local jurisdictions include Banfield, *Political Influence*; Martin et al., *Decisions in Syracuse.*

basis and receive their livelihood from private economic activity. The extent of business dealings among officials of municipal governments is an indicator of the interlocking character of the political system. The final channels of direct integration to be analyzed are the personal friendships of public officials. Such friendships, as a source of political integration, may well exist on the basis of similar personal interests, social rank and background, and because of the high personal mobility among the jurisdictions. Although a number of direct transaction measures have been enumerated, other random or chance contacts are always possible. It might happen, for example, that officials of different jurisdictions had an auto accident with each other. But other contacts would be largely unrelated to questions of political integration.

Political integration may occur through processes in which no direct contact is made between the governments or governmental officials of the separate jurisdictions, but occurs instead through some type of a political intermediary. Three different types of political intermediary systems of integration are examined. The first is the personal influence structure in the metropolitan area. Some private individuals may exert influence upon more than one of these municipalities, and in making demands upon separate jurisdictions, activities of those governments are made compatible.[34] At least two other para-political intermediary groups may exist for integrating activity between the formally autonomous jurisdictions. Interest groups abound in the Quad-Cities, and they may be making similar (or nonconflicting) demands upon the separate jurisdictions, facilitating political integration. Also, many of the major corporations are engaged in more than one of the cities. All the major industries draw workers and depend upon suppliers from throughout the area. These corporate interests (as distinguished from the associational groups) may also be making political demands upon the separate governments which serve to maintain the integration of the Quad-City political community.

While much literature exists upon "power structures" and decision-making in urban areas, very little of it deals systematically with these topics in an interjurisdictional manner.[35] In this study of the Quad-Cities, the con-

34. Martin et al., *Decisions in Syracuse*, pp. 338–341.
35. In William D'Antonio and William H. Form, *Influentials in Two Border Cities: A Study in Community Decision-Making* (South Bend: University of Notre Dame Press, 1965) the authors concern themselves with the influence structure of the international metropolitan area of El Paso and C. Juarez. But their primary emphasis is on a comparative study of influence in the two border cities, rather than a study of influence relationships in a single, binuclear metropolitan area. Forbes B. Hays, *Community Leadership* (New York and London: Columbia University Press, 1965) is advertised as a study of metropolitan or regional leadership in the New York area, but this is overstated. It is in fact, an interesting and useful historical analysis of the Regional Plan Association. Michael N. Danielson, *Federal-Metropolitan Politics and the Commuter*

cern is to develop indices of whether people, interest groups, or corporate interests, active and influential in the political life of the individual cities, are also active and influential in any of the other municipalities, or in the metropolitan area as a whole. An approach has been developed to get beyond the indeterminancy and unreliability of case study analysis, but which is not dependent on such an ethereal quality as reputation for influence. It may also be a useful technique for studying influence in other contexts, of course. One clear finding which emerges from the literature on community power is that results cannot be divorced from methods used in gathering information. For this reason, extended discussion of methodology will be deferred to the sections of this study which report the substantive findings on influential, interest group, and corporate activity among the municipalities of the Quad-City area.[36]

Another means by which activity may be integrated is through the actions of the news media serving the Quad-City area, and through the newsmen who cover municipal activities. The news media may serve as an information channel through which public officials learn what their counterparts are up to, and may also serve as a vehicle for implicit negotiation, through a process of statements to the press, followed by counterstatements.[37] The newsmen themselves may also be important intermediaries, as knowledgeable go-betweens. These activities of the news media and newsmen may function as a secondary process of political integration in the Quad-Cities.

Another potential channel may be found in the various municipal consultants which the separate jurisdictions employ. They are a type of private entrepreneur whose essential commodity is expertise. Engineering firms, planners, public administration research organizations, and bonding consultants all hold themselves out as advisors to municipalities in areas where the local governments do not possess the requisite "in-house" talent. To the extent that these consultants serve individually the different municipal governments in the Quad-City area, they can tap their own corporate intelligence about the activities and plans of the other municipalities, and thus integrate the programs of the separate jurisdictions.

The integrative functions of the news media and newsmen and the activities of the municipal consultants fit into a preliminary analysis of the

Crisis (New York: Columbia University Press, 1965) is a valuable case study of metropolitan politics, focusing upon interjurisdiction influence and action in the New York area. Many of the "classics" of power structure research have some interjurisdictional aspects, but such is not the focus of attention.

36. While this chapter gives a methodological overview of the Quad-City study, many particular technical problems will be discussed in the chapters in which the relevant substantive material is presented.

37. Holden, "The Governance of the Metropolis as a Problem of Diplomacy."

mutual adjustment of political activity which may occur in the Quad-City area without the need for either direct or indirect coordination. This is because "mutual adjustment" in this context requires, at a minimum, widespread knowledge among public officials of what activities other cities are undertaking.

The analysis focuses upon the extent to which public officials of the separate cities consciously take into account the activities of the other Quad-City municipalities in their own decision-making. It also assesses how much conscious specialization of services among the cities takes place within the metropolis, in which individual governments provide special services for the needs of the whole metropolitan population (or at least one larger than the service providing jurisdiction). Some of these services are the metropolitan airport, an art museum, bridges, and park facilities. Also taken into account is the extensiveness of the cities' borrowing of ideas and experiences from each other, and the frequency with which municipalities consciously make use of the experiences of their counterpart cities.

This is a most preliminary effort to make use of some of the insights of Lindblom's *The Intelligence of Democracy*. Two limitations upon this specification of Lindblom's ideas deserve special notation. First, the data for this analysis are the interview responses of the elected and appointed public officials. No effort is made to compare economies of scale which occur through specialization of services among separate municipalities over what might occur if governmental services were formally centralized or coordinated. It is implicit (when not explicit) throughout Lindblom's thesis that for some things mutual adjustment among autonomous decision-making groups is a more effective and efficient mechanism for the provision of services than is central coordination. This survey does not go beyond an assessment of just how much "mutual adjustment" consciously transpires among the public officials. Second, in relying upon responses of the public officials as the data, we necessarily rely upon *conscious* actions, at least in recall, while much of this type of activity may occur without any conscious awareness. For example, the simple process of "queuing up," in which decisions are made sequentially with each city's separate decisions taking place in a public environment composed of the prior decisions of the other cities, may well account for some integration of activity, but without anyone's conscious plan. Still, it is possible to point up a source of political integration which is usually not considered, but which may be important.

Conflict and conflict resolution are persistent themes in case study analyses of metropolitan politics. (Many of the studies of "intergovernmental relations," on the other hand, focus particularly on "cooperation.") The dramatic individual case reports may well present an exaggerated picture of the actual incidence of metropolitan conflict. Through the interview instrument, it has been possible to gather systematic evidence upon the incidence of interjurisdictional conflict in the Quad-City area. Following the suggestions of Holden,[38] this inquiry proceeds from the analysis of incidence to a study of the carry-over impact of conflicts upon other relations between the jurisdictions, and the acceptance of the resolution of disputes by the participants.

The following outline of the substantive material covered in this Quad-City study reflects the subject orientation of the study.

I. Interjurisdictional Agreements
II. Direct Interpersonal Transactions Among Public Officials
    A. Direct communication in the course of work
    B. Direct communication through municipal and professional associations
    C. Direct communication through social organizations
    D. Direct communication through political parties
    E. Direct communication through business dealings
    F. Direct communication through personal friendships
III. Indirect Activities as Processes of Integration
    A. "Influentials" as intermediaries
    B. Interest groups as intermediaries
    C. Major corporate interests as intermediaries
    D. News media and newsmen as intermediaries
    E. Consultants as agents of integration
IV. Mutual Adjustment of Political Activity Without Direct or Indirect Coordination
V. Conflict and Conflict Resolution

The study is designed to cover as many operative factors as possible in explaining the political integration of the Quad-City area. It is meant to get beyond case study emphasis on individual events, however significant, and is designed to offer hard data analysis upon *political structure*. Political structure means the *recurring patterns* of political action (covering all sorts of political events).

One omission in the study of processes of political integration should be specially noted, for it is a gap in this research, and its inclusion would require a wholly different approach. No effort is made to assess the impact of state law and other legal mandates which affect integration (except briefly as these touch upon specific processes of integration). State laws clearly impose many standardized and nonconflicting features upon municipal operations, even when "home rule" is granted and the municipalities operate in different states. Legal requirements surely make it more difficult,

38. Holden, "The Governance of the Metropolis as a Problem of Diplomacy."

in numerous ways, for one city to act in a manner which would undermine adjoining jurisdictions. This is potentially a part of the explanation of the continued healthy existence of metropolitan political systems. (It is often observed that state legal actions may promote fragmentation; it is not often discussed whether state law may also order the jurisdictional interstices.)

The data on transaction flows and all of the other measures analyzed in this study were gathered through a long structured interview schedule which was administered to the public officials in the Quad-City municipalities. There are questions about the reliability and interpretation of recall data of this kind, but more reliable ways to gather this type of information do not seem to be reasonably available. The methodological appendix discusses this problem and the assumptions made in this study. It also deals with technical questions of schedule construction and the statistical significance which can be attached to these findings. The respondents were the mayors, councilmen, department heads, and heads of boards and commissions of the ten cities. This was a population survey, and not a sample. The interview was actually administered to every one of the defined population, although in two instances respondents refused to answer some of the questions. The interviews commenced in the summer of 1966 and continued through the rest of the year.

By focusing upon quantitative indicators of political integration some other interesting and important subjects are omitted, or relegated to a secondary position. Very little systematic attention is devoted to the various subjects of transactions. This particular blinder is built into a "communications approach," although it is not rigidly adhered to where it interferes with important analysis in this study.

The study does not analyze power in the metropolis, nor does it deal with who benefits and who loses under this system. These are all essential questions to pursue, but here the purpose is solely to study the processes by which the political system of the Quad-City area is integrated and the political community is maintained.

A related limit of this study is that quantitative indicators lack the intrinsic interest which is aroused by a well-written case study. But case analysis has (or at least should have) about run its course in the study of metropolitan politics, although it can continue to give students the "feel" for the metropolis. It is past time when scholars should devote their skills to building upon this work by systematically studying the political structure of metropolitan areas. This book is an effort to do so.

The Quad-City area is a two-state metropolitan area, and one of seventy-one central cities of metropolitan areas which are within twenty miles of a state border, or commuting distance, so that interstate spillover consequences of municipal activity can be anticipated. Some studies of metropolitan political organization analyze interstate and even international areas, but the interstate or international part of the metropolis is frequently defined out of the study.[39] While it is commonplace to observe that many metropolitan problems do not observe state jurisdiction lines, this is often as far as analysis goes.[40] In this study the impact of the Mississippi River border will be a crucial variable.

The Quad-City area is multinuclear in its ecology, and is like many other metropolitan areas which have no one single dominant core city. Most metropolitan political analysis has focused upon single core cities and the outward radiating suburban communities, leaving political relationships in other types of metropolitan areas little explored. The ability of large cities particularly in close proximity to each other to get along and work jointly seems likely to become increasingly important as megalopolis and strip style urbanization proceeds.[41] Little consideration has been given to political relations between the large jurisdictions in megalopolis, despite the impending nature of this urban form.[42] The existing multinuclear metropolitan areas, such as the Quad-Cities, present an imperfect, but important laboratory for anticipating and exploring political and governmental service issues which will arise as large urban governments crowd in upon each other.[43]

A third advantage to the Quad-Cities as a research site is its size. The metropolitan area has a population in excess of 300,000. This size is important for two reasons. First, most analysis of metropolitan politics focuses upon the handful of giants. Usually the findings from studies in large metropolitan areas are simply presumed to be applicable in smaller areas. This

39. Bollens, *Exploring the Metropolitan Community*; Mowitz and Wright, *Profile of a Metropolis*. In *Federal-Metropolitan Politics and the Commuter Crisis*, Danielson presents a fascinating and suggestive case study of interstate metropolitan politics. My *Communications, Coordination and Control Among Local Governments in the Siouxland: A Study of Intergovernmental Relations*, includes an effort to systematically uncover some of the political relations in a three-state metropolitan area.
40. See the critique in Samuel K. Gove and Louis Silverstein, "Political Representation and Interstate Urban Agencies," *Illinois Government*, no. 17 (Urbana: Institute of Government and Public Affairs, University of Illinois, 1963).
41. Demographic predictions clearly envisage a great many more "strip" and "megalopolis" type developments. See, for example, Dennis McElrath, "Political and Social Implications of Urbanization," in *Proceedings of the 1964 Urban Policy Conference* (Iowa City: Institute of Public Affairs, University of Iowa), 24–32. Also see Jean Gottman, *Megalopolis* (New York: Twentieth Century Fund, 1961).
42. Richard Meier discusses "megalopolitan governments," which he envisions as systems of mutual arrangements, based upon the politics of negotiation in *Megalopolis Formation in the Midwest* (Ann Arbor: School of Natural Resources, University of Michigan, 1965).
43. Some journalists have noted the connection between the Quad-Cities and future megalopoli. "A megalopolis in miniature, the Quad-Cities of Iowa and Illinois may well be providing a preview of the great interurban complexes of the future," in "Mini-Megalopolis Rises Along the Mississippi," *Business Week*, February 25, 1967, pp. 168–170.

may not be true.[44] Three quarters of the metropolitan statistical areas as of the 1960 census had populations of under 500,000. Urban areas of this size deserve serious attention on their own.

A metropolitan area this size also presents a research advantage in that it is approachable. It became a major task to interview all mayors, councilmen, department heads and heads of boards and commissions of the area. It would be outlandish to conceive of doing this in the Chicago, Los Angeles or New York areas.

44. James G. Coke, "The Lesser Metropolitan Areas of Illinois," *Illinois Government*, no. 15 (Urbana: Institute of Government and Public Affairs, University of Illinois, 1962).

2

The Quad-City Area Organization

The Quad-City metropolitan region saddles the Mississippi at the upper rapids of the great river. These rapids are thoroughly tamed today, but in the past the hurdle they presented to river traffic had a lot to do with the early urban growth of the area.[2] From the earliest days, even before the arrival of white Americans, the pattern of settlement demonstrates a history of efforts at economic, social, and political integration within the area. The Sac Indian community of Saukenuk occupied the highlands of the present city of Rock Island for at least one hundred years before white settlement,[3] and may have been the largest permanent Indian community in existence in the Northwest Territory. In addition to the large main community at Saukenuk, there were smaller related villages at the present sites of Davenport and Moline.[4] These villages were politically and tribally united with Saukenuk and nominally controlled by the war chief Black Hawk at the time of white settlement, but conflict existed between the adjoining communities. The Indians living west of the Mississippi River seem to have sided with the early-day "Uncle Tom" of the Black Hawk War, Chief Keokuk, rather than follow Black Hawk. Notably, the militant Chief Black Hawk is widely honored today in the Quad-City area as a symbol of community identification, in contrast to the accommodating Chief Keokuk

1. This historical background relies heavily upon secondary reports and published reminiscences. Edward B. Espenshade, Jr., "Urban Development at the Upper Rapids of the Mississippi River" (Ph.D. diss., University of Chicago, 1944), is cited extensively.
2. Espenshade, "Urban Development." Also see Richard C. Wade, *The Urban Frontier* (Chicago: University of Chicago Press, 1959).
3. William A. Meese, "Indian History" in Newton Bateman and Paul Selby, eds., *Historical Encyclopedia of Illinois and History of Rock Island County* (Chicago: Munsell Publishing Co., 1914), p. 618.
4. "Indian History," *Historical Encyclopedia*, p. 618. For other primary sources see Espenshade, "Urban Development," p. 53.

who is not honored. From the fragmentary reports available from the past, it is possible that Black Hawk would feel somewhat familiar with the problems of political integration still existing among the present-day Quad-City area communities.

In 1816 a United States military fort was constructed on the lower end of Rock Island (now called Arsenal Island) which sits in the middle of the Mississippi River. Fort Armstrong was established to protect expected settlers and to control the Indians. It was also designed to safeguard river traffic between the settled areas on the lower Mississippi and the lead mining region around Dubuque and Galena, as well as support the important trade station and military fort at Prairie Du Chien. Settlement began almost immediately. Colonel Davenport, the fort sutler and a trader for Astor's American Fur Company, established the first trading post. Settlers began moving in on both sides of the river, as well as on to the island. By 1832 the community of Saukenuk was destroyed and the Sacs were removed to the West, as a result of the Black Hawk War. In the following ten years many of the Quad-City area communities were platted and created.

Davenport was established in 1836, and in 1841 the city of Rock Island was incorporated around the new courthouse, succeeding a smaller village. The Hampton agricultural community, upriver, had been in existence for some years by then, but lost out to Colonel Davenport's allies in a comic-opera dispute over the site of the county seat.[5] A ferry had connected the Davenport and Rock Island shores as early as 1825. Moline, established in 1843, was built in connection with the waterpower site on the inner channel of the Mississippi River (the Sylvan Slough) as it forked around Arsenal Island. Milan was also created in the 1840s, across the Rock River from Rock Island.

Many of the same people who were founders of Davenport were early leaders in Rock Island and to a lesser extent in Moline. All three of the original "tri-cities" can and do claim Colonel Davenport and Antoine Le Claire, in particular, among their founding fathers. Thus, evidence of an interlocking social system, at least among the leadership, can be found from the inception of the developing urban area which was initially focused around the military fort.

The early economic interdependence of the different communities is harder to document. As a site of a river transportation break, the communities around Rock Island and Davenport were competing for the up- and down-river traffic. Most vessels had to put in at one or the other city, in order to pick up a pilot and/or transship their goods around the rapids

5. Robert W. Olmsted, "County Organization and Government," in *Historical Encyclopedia*, pp. 636–645. Davenport had a similar "war" for governmental dominance with the now defunct village of Rockingham.

during the periods of low water. The hinterlands of the urban areas on both sides of the Mississippi River do not seem to have been a source of cross-river city competition. Davenport apparently served the Iowa hinterland, with Rock Island and Moline sharing the Illinois farmers' business. There is little evidence of commercial specialization in this preindustrial period which did not last long.

But when lumbermen set up sawmills in Rock Island and the other cities, as early as 1838, some functional specialization of the cities was foreshadowed. The lumber industry was located to serve the plains market, and large log booms or rafts were floated down the Mississippi from the north woods to the upper rapids area. The headquarters was clearly Rock Island. By the 1850s, the lumber business had become a big industry at the upper rapids, and it continued to grow for forty more years.[6] Moline's development was based upon its waterpower, and commenced when a mechanic, John Deere, established a small plow company there in 1847 to serve prairie farmers. Shortly thereafter Davenport began to establish its commercial hegemony of the urban area. It soon became the financial center for a large part of the new West.[7]

The commercial independence and even competitiveness of the three cities gave way to specialization and a symbiotic economic system by the middle of the nineteenth century. The upriver-downriver transportation break encouraged separate development initially, but the land transportation break the Mississippi created led to rather different consequences. Efforts to make transportation to the area less dependent upon the short Mississippi River season, and upon St. Louis, united the communities, as did the political struggle to bridge the Mississippi. Leaders from all three communities were involved in the long political struggle to get a franchise for the Rock Island Railroad. This effort culminated in success when the first train reached Rock Island in 1854.[8] It took an additional two years to bridge the Mississippi, for the political and judicial struggle was drawn out and complex, involving major sectional rivalry and many subplots. But leaders of the three cities of Davenport, Rock Island, and Moline recognized a common interest in the issue, and were able to work together. The

6. Espenshade, "Urban Development," pp. 70–74. See also John Clark Fetzer, A Study in City Building: Davenport, Iowa (Davenport: Davenport Chamber of Commerce, 1945), pp. 12–13.
7. See J. D. M. Burrows, Fifty Years in Iowa (Davenport: Glass and Co., 1888), reprinted in The Early Days of Rock Island and Davenport (Chicago: Lakeside Press, 1942), pp. 120–122; Espenshade, "Urban Development"; and Fetzer, A Study in City Building.
8. For a detailed account of this effort see Dwight L. Agnew, "Beginnings of the Rock Island Lines, 1851–1870" (Ph.D. diss., University of Iowa, 1947).

bridge, when built, established the tri-cities area as the major crossing point on the northern river.[9]

One other important event, having the character of an area defining issue, was the establishment of the Rock Island Arsenal. With pacification of the region, the military fort on the island became obsolete. It was decommissioned in 1838, became a military storage depot, and after many federal studies and much local effort the western arsenal was established on the island in 1862, right after the Civil War began. This crucial decision for the future of the area was predicated upon joint political activity by local interests. A committee composed of leading citizens from the tri-cities memorialized Congress, lobbied, produced and distributed maps and literature on the desirability of this location, and otherwise jointly promoted the site. The area interests were able to mobilize the two state congressional delegations, as well as the two state governments in the effort.[10] The Arsenal immediately began to promote the further integration of the urban area by drawing workers from all threee cities, and the government built foot and carriage bridges to the island linking the cities themselves in the process. The bridge system increased intercity contacts, previously dependent on a ferry system.[11]

During the next half century the tri-city area, as it was then called, developed into a major industrial complex. The lumber industry expanded along the lowlands at a rapid rate, until its precipitous decline just before the turn of the century. The farm implements industry also grew rapidly, but did not decline. The Arsenal's activity ebbed and flowed on an upward curve with the military requirements of the nation. New industries were established. The population grew steadily, if not spectacularly. The industrial area soon spilled over the corporate limits of the three large cities. As it did, new communities developed. East Moline, an industrial area along the Mississippi River, organized as a municipality in 1902. The result was one continuous Illinois urban belt from the railroad village of Hampton through East Moline, Moline, Rock Island, and across the Rock River to Milan. The Rock Island Line continued to expand, and around the extensive railroad yards in the river plain the community of Silvis developed. It was founded as a village in 1906, and was adjoined to East Moline. This linked the coal mining town of Carbon Cliff, founded in 1853, to the urban belt, and thus the seven Illinois communities which make up the statistical urbanized area have constituted a belt since the turn of the century. On the Iowa side of the Mississippi, Bettendorf was incorporated in 1903. It

9. Agnew, "Beginnings of the Rock Island Lines."
10. "Rock Island Arsenal," Historical Encyclopedia, pp. 830–840.
11. Espenshade, "Urban Development."

was an industrial and residential suburb, directly above Davenport, and grew around the present J. I. Case works, built in 1902.

All of this expansion during the last part of the nineteenth century and early years of the twentieth century was a continuation of the early growth of the area. No political decisions comparable to the fundamental decisions on the railroad, bridge, and arsenal were achieved in this period, but the governments and citizens were facing and resolving many of the problems of an extended multinuclear urban area.

An extensive metropolitan transportation system evolved during these years, and mutual aid agreements were effected among the cities' fire departments. Public improvements such as street lighting and paving were inaugurated early when compared to the introduction of such innovations in other areas. No one city of the three seems to have been the regular innovator.[12] It is reasonable to conjecture that the progressiveness of the three cities in this period is partly attributable to the close relationship of the cities to each other. Successful innovations were quickly emulated, and early journals and reports characteristically brag about how one city was the first to inaugurate some service or another, or provided it better, or cheaper, or more extensively than its sister cities. This competitiveness was probably not dysfunctional to the metropolitan area, for it probably stimulated the cities to introduce higher levels of municipal services at an earlier date, and provided a visible measure of progress to both officials and citizens of any one city.

Since the turn of the century the multinucleated metropolitan area has expanded and grown along lines already clearly established. Industry has further developed along the low Mississippi River floodplain. The cities and towns have grown; specialization has proceeded. One new municipality, Riverdale, Iowa, was created in 1950, largely at the instigation of Alcoa, which had built a major facility along the river, in a successful effort to avoid being annexed into Bettendorf. In addition to the Alcoa plant and some other industry, Riverdale has some residential development. By the 1930s, East Moline had grown into a large enough community so that people began referring to the area as the Quad-City area. In the 1950s, the industrial city of Bettendorf began a very rapid development as a bedroom community as well. It is now very common for residents to refer to the metropolitan area as the Quint-Cities. Three new automobile bridges now cross the Mississippi. Davenport built the first in 1936, which crosses between Bettendorf and Moline. In 1940, Rock Island built the second which crosses directly to Davenport, just below Arsenal Island. An interstate bridge was completed above the urbanized area in 1966. Davenport remains the largest city with the most commercial activity, while Rock

12. See the data in Espenshade, "Urban Development," pp. 88–90.

Island and Moline continue as industrial centers. Silvis focuses on the rail-yards, although a new John Deere foundry promises to make it look even more like a continuation of industrial East Moline. Hampton and Carbon Cliff now serve as small working-class suburbs without major industry or commercial activity. Milan continues as an autonomous community with its own commercial center, industrial and warehousing facilities, and a large number of bars and taverns which attract customers from throughout the area.

The major ethnic concentrations have been Germans, mainly on the Iowa side, and Swedish, on the Illinois side. Large Irish and Belgian groups are also found. Negroes are mainly concentrated in three areas of the Quad-Cities: in the inner-city part of Davenport, on the near west side of Rock Island, and in East Moline. A large Spanish-speaking community is also present in all of the major cities, with another concentration in Silvis.[13] Ethnically and racially the Quad-Cities are heterogeneous, as would be expected for a midwest industrial metropolitan region. Industry and working-class housing are located in the floodplain areas, and middle and upper-income housing in the hills, in the standard American pattern. What may be somewhat atypical is that all ten municipalities have lowlands and highlands. Thus, municipal borders have not become class or ethnic borders, although the mix of residents fluctuates from one municipality to another.

TABLE 1

1960 CENSUS FOR QUAD-CITY AREA MUNICIPALITIES

Jurisdiction	Population
Davenport	88,981
Rock Island	51,863
Moline	42,705
East Moline	16,732
Bettendorf	17,241*
Silvis	3,973
Milan	3,065
Carbon Cliff	1,268
Hampton	742
Riverdale	477

* Bettendorf census figures from special off year census conducted in 1965. Area planners indicate that all municipalities have experienced growth since 1960. In some cases population growth is estimated to be substantial.

13. For a discussion of settlement patterns of Negroes and Mexicans in the Quad-Cities see Lyle W. Shannon, "Economic Absorption and Cultural Integration of the Urban Newcomer" in *Emerging Problems in Housing and Urban Redevelopment* (Iowa City: Institute of Public Affairs, University of Iowa, 1965), pp. 24–46.

The twentieth-century development of the metropolitan area has required much governmental activity and political adjustment. The cities have expanded their borders, sometimes competitively. Since these political actions are part of this study and are not prologue, they will be discussed elsewhere.

THE METROPOLITAN COMMUNITY

Many of the historical events in the Quad-City area are shared experiences and occurred jointly to the municipalities. This common history is noteworthy because having joint historical experiences may be a key element in maintaining or creating an integrated community among formally autonomous units.[14] The joint history includes the Black Hawk War, the common frontier history, the Fort Armstrong and Arsenal activities, and a common relationship to the legendary Mississippi River. Perhaps the most important and impressive single, shared crisis for the Quad-City area in recent years was the Great Flood of 1965. The successful fight to control the flooding river was an experience shared by the residents of all ten municipalities. Having been a flood fighter is a proud remembrance, particularly for the high school and college students who are widely credited with actually saving the cities from terrible devastation.

This historical togetherness, of itself, would not develop a sense of metropolitan community. Past events would have to be remembered and celebrated, with each celebration serving to reinforce the sense of community, if historical events were to have contemporary integrative meaning. In the Quad-Cities a rich pattern of historical pageantry, memorials, and monuments may be found, which serve to symbolize the common historical past of the separate muncipalities. Area pageantry includes an annual Pow Wow held in Black Hawk State Park, in Rock Island, at the site of Black Hawk's "watchtower" on the bluff. Indian dancing and ceremonials are performed by the Sac-Fox remnants of Black Hawk's people. In 1966 the Fort Armstrong Sesquicentennial Committee (areawide) staged a pageant in honor of the 150th anniversary of the arrival of troops on the island. Each of the city newspapers gave the event wide notice, and the program was billed as celebrating "the birth of the Quad-Cities." In 1962 the Rock Island Arsenal celebrated its one hundredth anniversary with much ceremony.

The newspapers regularly print stories of local or area history, largely of an anecdotal nature. Such subjects as the historical clamming industry in the Quad-Cities (now reviving), riverboating on the Mississippi, and the great fires in the Quad-Cities are typical. Memorials and monuments are

14. Karl W. Deutsch, *Nationalism and Social Communication: An Inquiry into the Foundations of Nationalism* (Cambridge: M.I.T. Press, 1953).

also found. Plaques on the Memorial Bridge honor the young people who "saved our cities" in the 1965 flood, and college scholarships are provided for them. Black Hawk's village is now a state park, with his "watchtower" as the main attraction, and there is a nearby museum of early area history. Colonel Davenport's home, where he was murdered by the banditti, has been restored on Arsenal Island, in a part of the area-serving recreation facilities on the island. This homestead is advertised as the first to be built in the Quad-City area. The blockhouse of Fort Armstrong has been rebuilt on the island at its original site, and is close to the government bridge roadway. All of these important monuments, memorials, and museums stress the common and shared history of the metropolitan area. They are impressive and persistent reminders of the unity of the Quad-Cities.

A great many symbols of metropolitan community may also be found.[15] Perhaps the most notable symbols of community are the somewhat confused area identifications themselves. Up until the 1940s the area was generally referred to as the Tri-City area. One can almost date institutions by the area symbol they use. The Tri-City Symphony is an example of the earliest use. Many old-line commerical firms are still prefixed "Tri-City," and construction workers belong to the Tri-Cities Building Trade Council. The symbol Quad-City is numerically dominant. It is represented by such institutions as the Quad-City Metropolitan Airport, the Quad-City Angels (the minor league baseball team), the Quad-City Federation of Labor, the Quad-City Builders Association, and numerous others. Many of the newer commercial establishments refer to the Quint-Cities in their title, and radio stations identify themselves with the five-cities symbol. This symbol allows for the continuation of the same abbreviated area identification—"Q-C," which is the standard headline caption in the daily newspapers. One other symbol of limited area identification is found with some frequency in the designation "Mississippi Valley." Examples include the intercity and interstate high school athletic league; the Mississippi Valley Association of Evangelicals, which holds an annual prayer breakfast for mayors of Quad-City area municipalities; and the Mississippi Valley Pressman's Association, which holds an annual "Gridiron Dinner" for Quad-City area politicians, where the guests are lampooned in skits.

The symbol "Black Hawk" is used by many area institutions and firms. In addition it designates a state park and the community college. The symbolic use of the names of Antoine Le Claire and John Deere are also found throughout the area, pointing to a common past. Hotels, streets, commercial establishments and freeways use these symbols. Another set of symbols

15. For a valuable study of the meaning of symbols of community, see Richard L. Merritt, *Symbols of American Community, 1735–1775* (New Haven: Yale University Press, 1966).

frequently invoked are the bridges across the Mississippi. Line drawings and photographs of the bridges connecting the cities are found on all sorts of things. Tourist pennants, planning commission reports, industrial development brochures, postcards, and even publications of the individual city governments and chambers of commerce are regularly adorned with reproductions of the bridges. The bridges are landmarks and clearly symbols of the interdependence of the metropolitan area.

A related aspect of the Quad-City area deserving mention is what Kevin Lynch would refer to as the image of the metropolitan community.[16] While this author does not have Lynch's type of attitude and opinion data, nor the eye of an architectural critic, it is his opinion that from many vantage points in the Quad-Cities a comparatively clear image of an interdependent metropolis is conveyed and impressed upon an observer—no matter how cursory his observations. The casual walker along the Davenport levee, or along the less esthetically pleasing Rock Island levee, is impressed by the close relationships between the two cities, with the sharp edge of the bustling Mississippi, and with the connecting series of bridges across the river and to Arsenal Island. Because of the bluffs found throughout the area, there are many places from which an observer can see this area as a whole— particularly the relationship of Arsenal Island to the industrial and commercial lowlands spread out on both sides of the Mississippi. Lynch, in discussing the visual problems of metropolitan form, and the development of a metropolitan image writes:

> Dependence on a strong dominant element, while giving a much more immediate sense of relation and continuity, becomes more difficult as the environment increases in size, since a dominant must be found that is big enough to be in scale with its task, and has enough "surface area" so that all the minor elements can have some reasonably close relationship to it. Thus one needs a big river, for example, that winds enough to allow settlement to be fairly near its course.[17]

In the Quad-Cities the Mississippi River, with its bridges and large, open Arsenal Island centralizing the metropolitan area, seems to present just such a dominant motif. The Quad-City area as a metropolis seems to have a high degree of visual integrity, and this probably reinforces the values of metropolitan community, otherwise abundantly found among these adjoining municipalities.

This community which exists in the Quad-City area would appear to be rather rare among American metropolitan areas. It is common academic fare to assert that one of the problems in metropolitan areas is that a major

16. Kevin Lynch, The Image of the City (Cambridge: M.I.T. Press, 1960).
17. Lynch, The Image of the City, p. 113.

bifurcation occurs between jurisdictions sharing the same metropolitan place. Residents allegedly identify with their particular municipality, and fence out any commitment to the metropolis as a whole. If a lack of metropolitan identity and commitment is actually characteristic of American metropolitan areas, to that extent the Quad-City area is decidedly different. But this usual interpretation may be inadequate. One prominent student of American metropolitan affairs, Roscoe Martin, has even offered the Quad-City area as a chilling example of the lack of metropolitan identity!

> Al Smith was from the sidewalks of New York, not from the sidewalks of the New York-Northeastern New Jersey Standard Consolidated Area. Davenport-Rock Island-Moline is not a place name but a shelter designed to afford the statistician refuge from political fallout. The metropolitan area possesses no magic to stir men's souls; cities, si, SMSA's, no.[18]

Martin's view is drawn too casually, and its inapplicability is not much evidence against the general interpretation which he and others advance. Generally, the lack of commitment of metropolitan dwellers to their metropolitan area does not seem very clear, despite the assertions.

While the particular historical events in the Quad-Cities, and the other particular attributes of metropolitan community, are area specific, it seems quite possible that comparable measures could be found in many or even all American metropolitan areas. The Quad-City system may just be more surface apparent, due to the use of area identifications (Tri-City, Quad-City, Quint-City) which do not incorporate the name of the dominant city in the title.

It does seem that residents of cities and towns within metropolitan areas are often committed to the preservation of their separate municipal identities. This may be as true in the Quad-City area (as judged by public reactions to the proposed merger of Rock Island, Moline, and East Moline) as elsewhere. But identity with a municipality and with a metropolitan area are not necessarily zero-sum commitments. It is possible that a commitment to the local community can coexist with a commitment to the metropolis as a whole. Perhaps because reports on unification campaigns constitute a major part of the literature on metropolitan politics, commitment to municipality or metropolis has seemed to be competitive (with the

18. Roscoe Martin, *Metropolis in Transition: Local Government Adaptation to Changing Urban Needs* (Washington, D.C., H.H.F.A., 1963). Charles R. Adrian has a similar view of metropolitan identity: "There is no image of the 'good metropolitan life' outside of the writings of reformers and planners, none that stems from the grass roots, a latter day Jacksonianism, as a foundation upon which to build a political system. To the typical citizen, the metropolitan area is a place where his work is. It is not a community, but an aggregate of persons and places." In *Public Attitudes and Metropolitan Decision-Making,* Eighth Annual Wheritt Lecture on Local Government (University of Pittsburgh, 1962).

municipal commitment regularly winning out), but this is not necessarily the case.[19] In some ways the commitment to the separate municipalities may even be supportive of an area-wide identity. In the Quad-City area, for example, the pride and loyalty of the high school graduates to their own school of attendance is part of the area folklore, even if they live in a different city from that in which they graduated. Yet a fierce athletic rivalry probably is supportive of a Quad-City commitment, for all-star teams strive for the Quad-City championship, and sports reporters cover these athletic contests.[20]

In any event, in the Quad-City area, a commitment to the metropolitan community coexists with commitments to the local municipalities. This sense of metropolitan community probably supports and permits efforts at political coordination and intergovernmental actions between and among these cities. Occasionally it is asserted that intergovernmental transactions between local governments in metropolitan areas are most successful and frequent between administrative officials who shield these transactions from public view. This is purportedly because the public lacks the metropolitan orientation of the administrators, and would disapprove of such activity if they were aware of it.[21] In the Quad-City area, the existence of a feeling of metropolitan community permits and encourages municipal efforts to work cooperatively. It is not a hostile public environment. Many assertions exist in metropolitan literature which would seem to indicate that this is an unusual situation. But it may be more typical of American metropolitan areas than is generally believed.

MUNICIPAL GOVERNMENT ORGANIZATION

With some exceptions the ten municipal governments in the Quad-City area are providing most services normally associated with cities of their size. There is a lot of variation, in detail, among the muncipalities in the ways they are governmentally and politically organized. This is because municipalities are legal creatures of their state. Iowa and Illinois statutes differ

19. For an important introduction to conceptual problems of overlapping and multiple loyalties, see Harold Guetzkow, *Multiple Loyalties: Theoretical Approach to a Problem in International Organization* (Princeton: Princeton University Press, 1955).

20. Since so many people in the Quad-Cities live in a different city than where they grew up or went to school, it may not be too remote to suggest that the familiar "cross-pressure" hypothesis of voting research may be relevant in exploring the rarity of inter-city disputes, and the low-key of those disputes which do occur.

21. See, for example, Winston Crouch, "Conflict and Cooperation Among Local Governments in the Metropolis," *Annals* 359 (May 1965), 67; and John C. Bollens and Henry J. Schmandt, *The Metropolis: Its People, Politics and Economic Life* (New York: Harper & Row, 1965), p. 373.

from each other, but both states provide only a small variety of organizational options to their municipalities. Despite organizational dissimilarities, all but one of the ten operate under some variation of the mayor-council type of government.[22] Rock Island is the exception. It operates under a council-manager system, but with an elected mayor.

The municipalities show a wide variety of partisan orientations. Davenport and Moline are traditionally Republican, and currently have Republican mayors and large Republican majorities on their councils.[23] Rock Island is ostensibly nonpartisan, although its officers are mostly Republicans. Partisanship is quite muted in city affairs. East Moline is solidly Democratic. All of the smaller Illinois municipalities have mayors and councils which are Democratically oriented, although some also have local parties. Bettendorf operates under an unusual system for Iowa, although common enough elsewhere. Two local parties, which do not bear any one-to-one relationship to the national parties, compete for election. Riverdale, Iowa, is nonpartisan, de facto as well as de jure. In keeping with the social status of most residents, however, the majority of the council and the mayor are Republican.

The major cities provide the full gamut of "caretaker" services, and many other activities of cities in their size range.[24] Rock Island has the only federal urban-renewal project currently under way, but Davenport, Moline, East Moline, and Milan are all presently contemplating such programs. In Davenport and Bettendorf water is provided by a private company. The

22. Many small municipalities in Illinois, legally "villages," operate under what is called a "trustee" system, in which, legally, there is no mayor. The trustees are led by a "president of the board of trustees." Elected separately, this officer operates as, and is frequently called "mayor." The system is used in Milan, Carbon Cliff, and Hampton.
23. Davenport is the only major Iowa city which operates with a partisan system having national parties designated on the ballot. This occurs because Davenport operates under a "special charter," granted before the present statutory municipal requirements were enacted. For a discussion of Iowa laws on municipal elections see George B. Mather, A Citizen's Guide to Iowa Municipal Government and Elections (Iowa City: Institute of Public Affairs, University of Iowa, 1959). For a discussion of elections and partisanship in Illinois municipalities see Samuel K. Gove, "Local Government and Local Politics" in Myra Lynch, ed., Illinois Local Government, 2nd ed. (Urbana: Institute of Government and Public Affairs, University of Illinois, 1965), pp. 28–40.
24. For a useful analysis of the services provided in Rock Island, Moline, and East Moline see the J. L. Jacobs Company report to the Joint City Unification Committee, Feasibility of the Unification of City Governments of Rock Island, Moline and East Moline (Chicago: August 1965) and the supplementary report, October 1965. For a similar, consciously modeled report on Silvis municipal activities, see the unpublished council memorandum "Financial and Social Impact of Unification of Silvis and East Moline," (1966). Davenport's municipal activities are analyzed in Harry R. Smith and Fred Sudermann, A Survey of Municipal Organization and Administration—Davenport, Iowa (Iowa City: Institute of Public Affairs, University of Iowa, 1961).

Some comparative data on tax structures, service levels, etc., of the Quad-City municipalities is found in the J. L. Jacobs report, and the regularly updated publication of the Iowa–Illinois Industrial Development Group, A Prospectus of the Quad-City Area (Rock Island).

other large cities have municipal systems, as do most of the smaller municipalities. (Riverdale is served by a small private company connected to the Alcoa interests, and Hampton purchases water from East Moline.) Municipal library systems are provided in the five large cities and in Silvis. All municipalities have fire departments except Milan, which is included within the Black Hawk Fire Protection District. East Moline does not have a municipal recreation program comparable to the other large cities, but the city is served by a recreation program supported by the United Fund. Moline and Rock Island operate low-rent public housing projects. Moline operates the only municipal hospital, and the only municipal cemetery. On both sides of the river public education is carried on by independent governments, and public welfare is a county function. Davenport, Rock Island, and Moline have the only milk inspection programs. Bridge commissions in Davenport and Rock Island have built and operate interstate toll bridges. Davenport has the only municipal art gallery. Rock Island, Moline, and East Moline are within the Quad-City Metropolitan Airport Authority District. Each mayor appoints one member to the administrative board of the metropolitan airport. Davenport maintains a small separate municipal airport. The three smallest municipalities (Carbon Cliff, Hampton, and Riverdale) provide essential caretaker services, and little more. Riverdale, for example, with the large Alcoa property, has yet to levy a tax rate of one mill!

These differences in services among the municipalities are important to note for at least two reasons. First, municipalities which do not provide a service seem unlikely to have intergovernmental activity concerning that service. (But municipalities contemplating some activity may rely on experiences of adjoining municipalities.) Second, it is important to consider whether through some reciprocal process, the cities achieve economies of scale by not duplicating services in which one installation would serve the metropolitan area.

Throughout the history of the Quad-City area there have been efforts to unify cities. The most recent effort has been a proposal to unify the cities of Rock Island, Moline, and East Moline. This move was initiated by some chamber of commerce members and has had the backing of John Deere and Company and the Iowa-Illinois Gas and Electric Company, two major corporations with interests in all three cities. The proposed unification would retain the present cities as "boroughs," but without local authority, and a city-manager system would be established.[25]

25. This discussion relies heavily upon personal interviews with Charles Iseley, Jr., and John Hollingsworth. Mr. Iseley has kindly permitted access to his extensive files on the unification campaign. In addition to the Jacobs Report, the League of Women Voters of Rock Island have issued their own report, "What Do You Need to Know About the Possible Unification of Our Cities?" (November 1965). All of these sources should be specially absolved of any complicity in the interpretations offered here.

A unification committee commissioned a "feasibility study" by the J. L. Jacobs Company of Chicago. The study supported the preliminary recommendations of the unification committee in a report issued in August 1965. Since then, after an initial flurry of publicity and activity through the early months of 1966, the proposal has remained dormant. Some backers insist that the issue is still alive—only awaiting proper timing. Permissive special legislation has been passed in the Illinois legislature for a referendum.

The unification effort is an interesting event because it seems to be an anachronism. Many observers believe that the reform movement to unite metropolitan areas has finally run its failure-studded course.[26] The publication of the Jacobs Report brought rather predictable public responses from city officials. Most have been noncommittal or politely critical of the report in public. In private conversations, many are considerably more critical of both the recommendations and the factual assertions and analysis by the Jacobs Company. This whole unification effort points up the fact that many influential people have been unhappy with the present political organization of cities in the Quad-City area. They have felt that there are too many governments with overlapping responsibilities.[27] In this regard, the public dialogue about the jungle-like quality of governmental service activities in the metropolitan area is much the same as reported in other metropolitan areas. Frequent newspaper stories about annexation disputes between the different cities reinforce this view.

A surface view of municipal government activity in the Quad-City area might very well lead an observer to conclude that the cities each tend to go their own way, with little coordination of effort. But this familiar enough view of metropolitan political life would not explain how the cities have managed to grow, to build integrated road systems, to avoid unacceptable spillover conditions, and generally to survive as separate jurisdictions for all of these years in the governmentally crowded environment at the upper rapids of the Mississippi.

26. See Henry J. Schmandt, "Changing Directions," *National Civic Review* 54 (November 1965), 530–534; and "The Emerging Strategy," *National Civic Review* 55 (June 1966), 325–330.
27. A meeting was held on the CED study entitled *Modernizing Local Government* (New York: July 1966), and its application in the Quad-City area. Some 200 Quad-City leaders attended, including the mayors of the large cities. For a report see *New York Times*, February 27, 1967, p. 43.

3

Interjurisdictional Agreements

STUDYING INTERJURISDICTIONAL AGREEMENTS

Direct agreements between the political jurisdictions within metropolitan areas are one of the organizational tools which governments may use in providing coordinated political and governmental services to their residents. Most catalogs of potential remedies for perceived problems within the American metropolis list interjurisdictional agreements as one of the partial remedies.[1]

The extensiveness of the use of the organizational device of interjurisdictional agreements within metropolitan areas remains somewhat problematical. Notwithstanding a paucity of analysis,[2] interpretations about the

---

1. The classic catalog is, Victor Jones, *Metropolitan Government* (Chicago: University of Chicago Press, 1942). For recent modifications see Jeptha J. Carrell, "Learning to Work Together," *National Municipal Review* 43 (November 1954), 526; Roscoe Martin, *Metropolis in Transition: Local Government Adaptation to Changing Urban Needs* (Washington, D.C.: H.H.F.A., 1963); Advisory Commission on Intergovernmental Relations, *Alternative Approaches to Governmental Reorganization in Metropolitan Areas* (Washington, D.C., 1962).

2. Interjurisdictional agreements are not unexplored, but much of the analysis has been published as rather fugitive literature—the output of bureaus and citizens groups, or in unpublished theses. W. Brooke Graves' compendium, *American Intergovernmental Relations* (New York: Charles Scribner's Sons, 1964) provides a valuable overview of this literature (Chapter 21, "Interlocal Relations," 737–779). One useful publication which Graves's net missed is Matthew Holden, *Intergovernmental Agreements in the Cleveland Metropolitan Area*, a staff report to the Study Group on Governmental Organization, Cleveland Metropolitan Service Commission, 1958.

One type of interlocal agreement, in one area, which has received extensive coverage is the so-called "Lakewood Plan," used in the Los Angeles area, where municipalities contract with the county government to provide urban services. See Samuel K. Gove, *The Lakewood Plan* (Urbana: University of Illinois, 1961); Winston Crouch, *Intergovernmental Relations*, Metropolitan Los Angeles Study, vol. 15 (Los Angeles: Haynes Foundation, 1954), 59–84; Winston Crouch and Beatrice Dinerman, *Southern California Metropolis: A Study in Development of Government for a Metropolitan Area* (Berkeley and Los Angeles: University of California Press, 1964), pp. 199–205.

potential for such agreements are reasonably well crystallized among political scientists dealing with metropolitan problems.

Interjurisdictional agreements are commonly interpreted to be peripheral devices, perhaps useful in facilitating some rather minor activities; but because of inherent limitations, they are not major integrating mechanisms for the metropolitan polity (this excepts some interpretations of the "Lakewood Plan"). Interjurisdictional agreements are still considered to be useful in a limited way however, because of the relative ease with which they can be adopted.[3] Recently there have been some academic efforts to use interjurisdictional agreements as indicators of political integration. These efforts provide a wealth of methodological cues, and some important evidence, although they avoid analysis of the service payoffs realized through contractual arrangements.[4]

The status of interjurisdictional agreements between and among the ten municipalities of the Quad City area are explicated in this chapter. Some interpretations given here are at variance with interpretations of other students of interjurisdictional agreements. Consequently, it seems desirable to distinguish the classification decisions (which were made in this part of the Quad-City study) as a part of the corpus of this chapter rather than in an appendix. The particular approach used in the Quad-City study undoubtedly contributes to the divergence of findings at least as much, and probably considerably more, than the difference between the political structure in the Quad-City area and the political structure in the Cleveland, Philadelphia, or the other metropolitan areas which have been analyzed.

In the Quad-City survey both the so-called formal contractual agreements and the informal agreements concerning services have been classified as a single group. This is similar to the system that Jeptha Carrell used in the Philadelphia area study,[5] but is different from most other measures which have been gathered. Most surveys of interjurisdictional agreements have either limited themselves to formalized contracts or have treated formal contracts and informal agreements as being different *in esse*.

3. See John C. Bollens and Henry J. Schmandt, *The Metropolis: Its People, Politics and Economic Life* (New York: Harper & Row, 1965), pp. 371–392. This excellent book is a reasonably accurate litmus paper test of what the best standard current thinking is on any particular issue of metropolitan import. See also the ACIR Report, *Alternate Approaches to Governmental Reorganization in Metropolitan Areas*, 26–33; Matthew Holden, *Interjurisdictional Agreements in the Cleveland Metropolitan Area*, 37.
4. See James V. Toscano, "Transaction Flow Analysis in Metropolitan Areas: Some Preliminary Explorations," in Phillip E. Jacob and James V. Toscano, eds., *The Integration of Political Communities* (Philadelphia and New York: J. B. Lippincott, 1964) pp. 98–119; Thomas R. Dye et al., "Differentiation and Cooperation in a Metropolitan Area," *Midwest Journal of Political Science* 7 (May 1963), 145–155; Charles S. Liebman et al., "Social Status, Tax Resources, and Metropolitan Cooperation," *National Tax Journal* 16 (March 1963), 56–62.
5. Jeptha J. Carrell, "Learning to Work Together," 527.

The reason for the Quad-City classification is that from the preliminary analysis of completed interview schedules no substantial difference in the compelling character of the formal as opposed to informal agreements was found, nor was any reasonable breaking point found between the type of services covered by informal arrangements and the type formalized into a contract. Obviously, most agreements involving very major capital expenditures were formalized, but many less major agreements were also formalized. Even some rather important agreements remain unformalized. For example, mutual aid fire agreements interlace this metropolitan area. Some have been formalized while some have not. Both types of agreement compel performance. No fire chief in the area could recall any incidents in which requests for service had not resulted in a response. There appears to be no substantial behavioral difference between formal or informal mutual aid fire agreements in the Quad-City area. Similarly, some maintenance agreements concerning boundary roads are formally agreed upon while others are not. Once again there are no perceptible differences in performance. The only contemporary agreement in this whole area in which there has been any subsequent issue concerning adequacy of performance is an agreement between Silvis and Carbon Cliff whereby Silvis has located its disposal plant within the adjoining community. Carbon Cliff argues that the plant emits noxious smells which Silvis refuses to correct. This agreement is formalized although its legality is somewhat obscure and may be litigated.

There is a serious question whether "formal"/"informal" is a very clear-cut dichotomy. It surely is not for many of the metropolitan political actors who cannot characterize their own arrangements. The legal basis for a great many of these relationships, if any, has often disappeared into the hazy past, before any of the current governmental actors were around. The lack of saliency of "formal"/"informal" is further attested by the inability of many of the respondents to even know where to look to find out about the kind of a relationship. Even when the genesis of an agreement can be established, the characterization is often still difficult. Consider the agreement among the five major police departments to exchange arrest data. No written contract or agreement seems to exist. However, the procedure is spelled out to the point of routinization with each department. Written forms are exchanged; the procedures are followed. Does this constitute a "formal agreement?" Perhaps not.[6] In any case, it seemed that it was a better measure of political integration to treat each of such ripened understandings as a transaction, without regard to its "formal" or "informal" character. Measures which only deal with the "formal" agreements seem inappro-

6. Usually the distinction between "formal" and "informal" seems to be made upon the basis of whether or not a *written* and *signed* agreement exists. A *written* and *signed* agreement is a "formal" one. But some of the so-called "informal" agreements (un-

priate as indicators of political integration, or as indicators of service agreements in operation between the jurisdictions.

The survey of agreements in operation was conducted as part of the interview of all mayors, councilmen, department heads, and heads of boards and commissions in all ten municipalities in the Quad-Cities. Each department or agency head was asked to list any agreements in which his department or agency had participated. (This was asked separately for formal and informal agreements, and the responses were grouped.)

In almost all other surveys the data was apparently gathered (but not always indicated) by means of a mailed questionnaire sent to the various governments. Apparently some one individual city official became the respondent. It was determined that this would be unsatisfactory for this study from the preliminary round of discussions with city clerks, mayors, and other key informants in the Quad-City municipalities. No one municipal official in these cities had accurate information as to what agreements his own government was committed. Nor was it possible for these officials to turn to any central file which contained this information. They seemed to be about as unaware of some of the "formal" agreements as the "informal" ones. These officials did not even recall or have any records on agreements the interviewers already knew about from recent reports in the press.

An analysis of these preliminary responses indicated that in the Quad-City area only the librarians had knowledge of some of the interlibrary arrangements. Only the streets departments could be relied upon to know about the existence of boundary road service agreements. Only the police chiefs could respond to questions concerning police agreements, and so on down the line. Even a department head's responses could not always be taken at face value. Other surveys, which rely upon mailed responses of one city official for his city, seem likely to miss a very substantial part of the cooperative texture of relationships between governments in metropolitan areas, even when that is the direct purpose of their survey.[7]

written) seem to possess all the attributes of legally binding contracts. They may be just as enforceable in court, even if unwritten. They seem to evidence all the requirements of legal contracts (mutual intent, consideration, legal capacity, etc.). On the other hand, in many of these instances, whether all the elements of enforcible contracts are present is a close question, which could only be decided if someone took the case to court. (Such has not happened in the Quad-City area during the period of research, nor did any of our respondents call our attention to any such action in the past.) This almost hopelessly snarls any effort to characterize agreements upon the basis of their legal enforcibility.

7. Surveys which limit themselves to some one particular kind of agreement, or only involve intergovernmental transfers of funds, are more likely to be reasonably accurate, in that it is probably possible to locate the particular type of respondents who will have the required information (or the particular records). Thus, I do not on this account challenge the accuracy of Jacob's data in Jacob and Toscano, eds., *The Integration of Political Communities*, or some of the counts of Lakewood style agreements in the Los Angeles area.

Even the gathering of data by means of personal probing interviews does not present an entirely reliable listing of the interjurisdictional agreements which exist. The very existence of an agreement is sometimes "foggy" to the participants. Upon a number of occasions one party to a purported "agreement" would inform the interviewer about it, but his counterpart would not list it. Often the interviewer could clear this up by raising the "agreement" to the "nonremembering" respondent, if the interviewer happened to be briefed concerning a prior counterpart interview. When time permitted, discrepancies were checked. But enough forgetfulness came to the surface, even with probing and searching of documents, that it is entirely possible that some agreements actually exist and are in force and which *neither* of the two responsible department heads recalled to the interviewers. Through newspaper accounts an emergency storm alert agreement was uncovered, for example, among some of the jurisdictions. None of the responsible civil defense directors mentioned this agreement, although they had met and modified it within the past year. The respondents also appeared about as likely to forget the existence of a "formalized" agreement as a less formal one.

In coding the interviews some other discrepancies in the responses first appeared. A coding decision was made, consistent with other coding decisions in this survey, that any respondent who *listed* an agreement with another jurisdiction, would be believed over his counterpart's not listing of that agreement. It seems very obvious that some of these officials did not recall agreements that were in operation. On the other hand, little reason appeared which would suggest that respondents would be likely to "remember" agreements which, in fact, did not exist.

The agreements which have been classified are all of an ongoing nature. Single event accords in which the "contract" has been fulfilled are omitted. Thus an alternate year maintenance agreeement is listed, but the fact of one city installing a stop sign on a border drive with the other city providing the sign is not counted if it was simply an agreement to solve the single service problem when it arose. Similarly the arrangement that Davenport, Rock Island, Moline, and Bettendorf parks and recreation people meet each spring to fix the salaries they will offer seasonal employees, as well as other matters, is classified as an agreement, while the arrangement between some Bettendorf and Moline officials one year, both interviewing the same set of prospective employees, that they would not try to outbid each other, and would only offer jobs after agreement first between themselves as to who offers a job to which recruit, is obviously not an interjurisdictional agreement in this sense. These types of short span cooperations are so frequent as to be almost uncountable, although they are usually not as interesting as in this example.

These difficulties in classification have not been discussed in many of the reports which are available. It is not clear how these problems have been resolved. One suspects that in some instances no effort was made to relate and compare the responses of jurisdictions to test for consistency. Perhaps some of these studies have abdicated the classification task to the individual judgments of the respondents, thus submerging the difficulty. But usually the steps taken in gathering and classifying data are not spelled out.[8]

EXTENT AND PATTERN OF AGREEMENTS

The extensiveness of interjurisdictional agreements in the Quad-City area is much higher than could be anticipated. Among themselves, the ten municipalities have a total of 252 identified agreements.[9]

This count is substantially more than could be anticipated from research reports on other metropolitan areas. In Philadelphia, among some 686 local jurisdictions, Jeptha Carrell registered surprise at finding as many as 756 agreements.[10] If it is presumed that these agreements were all bilateral, that would amount to an average of just over two per jurisdiction. In the Quad-City area the average is just over fifty per city, and this classification is only among the ten municipalities. No count is included of agreements between any of these ten municipalities and any other local jurisdiction in the region.

While this extensive network of interjurisdictional accords was not anticipated, the distribution of agreements was not expected to be random. It was hypothesized that the larger jurisdictions would be involved in more intergovernmental agreements than the smaller ones.[11] It was also expected that the state border intersecting the metropolitan area would affect the distribution of agreements.[12] Interjurisdictional agreements were predicted

8. Matthew Holden is a clear exception. He notes some of the same problems, and explains his procedures in resolving them in *Intergovernmental Agreements in the Cleveland Metropolitan Area.*
9. Whenever a multilateral agreement was encountered, it was broken into its component bilateral agreements. Thus, a multilateral milk inspection agreement between Davenport, Rock Island, and Moline was coded as three bilateral agreements (Davenport–Rock Island, Davenport–Moline, and Rock Island–Moline).
10. Carrell, "Learning to Work Together," 526. In commenting on Carrell's study, W. Brooke Graves considers this many agreements "astonishing" (Graves, *American Intergovernmental Relations,* p. 746).
11. This seems to be a consistent finding. See the review in Graves, *American Intergovernmental Relations.*
12. State borders are generally considered to present serious, if not insurmountable barriers to interjurisdictional agreements. See Daniel R. Grant, "The Government of Interstate Metropolitan Areas," *Western Political Quarterly* 8 (March 1955), 90–107.

to be overwhelmingly between contiguous municipalities.[13] As will be seen, these hypotheses cannot be entirely accepted for the Quad-City area.

TABLE 2

DISTRIBUTION OF INTERJURISDICTIONAL AGREEMENTS FOR EACH
MUNICIPALITY IN THE QUAD-CITY AREA

Jurisdiction	Number
Davenport	77
Rock Island	92
Moline	96
East Moline	83
Bettendorf	64
Silvis	52
Milan	23
Carbon Cliff	4
Hampton	3
Riverdale	10

The distribution of agreements varies substantially for these municipalities, as Table 2 indicates. While the mean for interjurisdictional agreements is 50.5 per city, Moline is a party to 96 agreements, to lead the way. Hampton is only involved in three interjurisdictional agreements. The five larger cities average about 82 agreements per city, while the five smaller ones average only slightly more than 16 per municipality. Thus, the five larger cities are parties to approximately six times the number of agreements than those involving the five smaller municipalities.

The largest number of interjurisdictional agreements are among the five largest cities (Davenport, Rock Island, Moline, East Moline, and Bettendorf). The small-municipality to small-municipality agreements are so few as to be negligible. Most of the agreements to which small municipalities are a part are with one of the five larger jurisdictions.

TABLE 3

DISTRIBUTION OF INTERJURISDICTIONAL AGREEMENTS AMONG
DIFFERENT SIZED JURISDICTIONS IN THE QUAD-CITY AREA

Type of Relationship	Number
Big city–big city	167
Big city–small municipality	78
Small municipality–small municipality	7
	252

13. Some recent studies in the Philadelphia area simply assume that noncontiguous contractual relations are not extensive or important. See Dye, "Differentiation and Cooperation in a Metropolitan Area."

This distribution deserves reflection. It seems clear that there are few, if any, occasions in the Quad-City area in which two or more of the small, resource-poor jurisdictions pool their limited resources through an agreement, in order to jointly provide that which neither of them could singly provide. (It seems reasonable to assume that the larger jurisdictions possess resources which enable them to provide many services, while the small jurisdictions do not. Riverdale, Iowa, is something of an exception. With its large Alcoa plant and relatively prosperous housing, it obviously has tremendous local resources.) The small jurisdictions frequently participate with and receive services from some larger jurisdiction. In most of these relationships the large municipality's contribution is a quite small increment to its other activity, but the small jurisdiction receiving the service tends to rely heavily on that service. A type of satellite-sun relationship seems to exist between these small municipalities and their larger neighboring jurisdiction.[14] This distribution, with numerous big city to small jurisdiction agreements, and almost no small jurisdiction to small jurisdiction ones, also raises some interesting points concerning the supposed propensity of small suburban jurisdictions within metropolitan areas to ally themselves against their larger urban neighbors.[15] There is little visible evidence of any such an alliance system in the Quad-City area today, or in the recent past. But in other metropolitan areas these alliances have seemed to spring to life in response to specific major issues: a unification campaign in the St. Louis area, a commuter crisis in the New York area, or a core city imposed income tax on suburban residents working in Detroit. In the Quad-City area it is apparent that there is not a substantial infrastructure of agreements between the small jurisdictions which would lay the groundwork through this type of patterned cooperation for joint action on specific major issues. Other relationships among the small jurisdictions will be discussed elsewhere in the Quad-City study.

These agreements, particularly among the five large cities, are frequently hidden from view. It seems clear, for example, that each mayor of the larger

14. The existence of the satellite-sun system becomes more complicated when the agreements between small municipalities and large cities are examined separately. Silvis, substantially more integrated (on the basis of its agreements) to the larger municipalities than the other small jurisdictions, does not fit this mold. Its near neighboring large jurisdiction is East Moline. Only 12 agreements exist between these two. This is more than with any other single jurisdiction, but Silvis is a party to 52 agreements. Milan, adjoining Rock Island, and close to Moline, has six agreements with Rock Island, five with Moline, and 13 with all other jurisdictions. Carbon Cliff, adjoining none of the larger cities has all four of its agreements with the adjoining and more urban and larger Silvis. Hampton has all three of its agreements with East Moline. Riverdale, a party to ten agreements, has five with adjoining Bettendorf. But these figures understate the satellite-sun relationship, because the "satellite to sun" agreements tend to be direct bilateral agreements, while a great many of the other relations between small jurisdictions and the large cities are as part of multilateral obligations involving many jurisdictions.
15. See, for example, Crouch and Dinerman, *Southern California Metropolis*.

cities would be surprised to read about the extensiveness of obligations to which his own city is committed.

An important question in assessing the value and importance of inter-municipal agreements (or other integrative mechanisms) within many metropolitan areas concerns intersecting state boundaries. The problem of surmounting this difficulty has perplexed political scientists who have considered it. The different state laws affecting local governments, a frequently perceived "poor neighbor" policy across state lines and a lack of legal authority, are all listed as placing serious barriers in the way of interjurisdictional agreements or other joint efforts of municipalities across state lines.[16]

In the Quad-City area there are a substantial number of interjurisdictional agreements which do cross the Mississippi River line. Out of 252 interjurisdictional agreements among the ten municipalities, 97 are between parties on the opposite side of the Mississippi River from each other. Whatever the barriers to interjurisdictional agreements across state lines, they are not unbreachable.

If interjurisdictional agreements are distributed with equiprobability, for comparison, it is possible to begin to see what impact the state boundary has upon the likelihood of jurisdictions entering agreements. Because there are seven jurisdictions in Illinois and only three in Iowa, if the agreements were distributed evenly there would be slightly more intrastate agreements than interstate. With 45 different potential sociometric partner relationships among the ten municipalities, 24 are intrastate, while 21 are interstate. If interjurisdictional agreements were distributed evenly, then, 53⅓ per cent would be intrastate while 45⅔ per cent would be interstate. Table 4 compares the number of interjurisdictional agreements which would be expected to be intrastate and interstate if they were distributed with equiprobability, and the actual distribution of agreements found in the Quad-City area. As expected, intrastate agreements are very much more common than interstate ones. The border is a substantial barrier. Nonetheless, interstate interjurisdictional agreements are much more frequent than was initially anticipated.

TABLE 4

EXPECTED AND ACTUAL DISTRIBUTION OF INTERSTATE AND INTRASTATE
INTERJURISDICTIONAL AGREEMENTS IN THE QUAD-CITY AREA

	Interstate	Intrastate
Expected	118	134
Observed	97	155
		N = 252

16. Grant, "The Government of Interstate Metropolitan Areas." See also John M. Winters, *Interstate Metropolitan Areas* (Ann Arbor: University of Michigan Legal Publications, 1962); and Graves, *American Intergovernmental Relations*, Chapter 20.

When the transactions among the five large cities are examined, we see that the same pattern appears. Among themselves the five large cities participate in 167 transactions. Seventy-seven are interstate, as compared to 90 intrastate. Of the ten sociometric possibilities, six are interstate and four intrastate. So if transactions were equally distributed 60 per cent of them (100) would cross the Mississippi, while 40 per cent (67) would not. Table 5 compares the expected and observed interstate and intrastate interjurisdictional agreements among the five large cities.

TABLE 5

EXPECTED AND ACTUAL DISTRIBUTION OF INTERSTATE AND
INTRASTATE INTERJURISDICTIONAL AGREEMENTS AMONG
THE FIVE LARGE CITIES IN THE QUAD-CITY AREA

	Interstate	Intrastate
Expected	100	67
Observed	77	90
		N = 167

Among the five larger cities, the Mississippi River state boundary is a highly significant barrier to interjurisdictional agreements. Once again, however, the astonishing thing, in view of assertions in the literature, is that as many as 77 interjurisdictional agreements do cross the state line. Interstate interjurisdictional agreements among the large cities are less frequent across the state line than within the same state, but they are very common.

One important variable which has not yet been introduced may affect these results. Contiguity has often been asserted or assumed to be very important in explaining the distribution of interjurisdictional agreements. Thomas Dye writes, "While not absolutely essential, local governments must generally be contiguous for cooperation to be feasible."[17]

That assessment overstates the need for contiguity. In the Quad-City area, out of 252 interjurisdictional agreements, 121, or close to half, are between parties which are not contiguous to each other. None the less physical contiguity may explain a good deal of the differentiation in the volume of interjurisdictional agreements between interstate and intrastate partners.

Of the 45 possible jurisdictional ties in the Quad-City area, ten are between contiguous jurisdictions (including contiguous jurisdictions across the river from each other) and 35 are between noncontiguous jurisdictions. Thus 22 per cent of the agreements would be expected to be between con-

17. Dye, "Differentiation and Cooperation in a Metropolitan Area."

tiguous partners and 78 per cent (197) between noncontiguous ones, if the agreements were distributed equally. In fact agreements between contiguous jurisdictions are close to two and one-half times as frequent as could be expected. Contiguity is related to the frequency of interjurisdictional agreements. Among the five large jurisdictions five contiguous and five noncontiguous relationships are possible. This means that the 167 agreements should be split evenly (83.5), if it is assumed that contiguity is a null factor. In fact 101 contiguous agreements are in operation, while 67 noncontiguous ones were found. Thus, among the large cities, contiguous agreements account for far less than they do for all jurisdictions, but are still more common than could be expected if agreements were equally distributed.

Among the five large jurisdictions five contiguous relationships are possible (Davenport–Rock Island, Davenport–Bettendorf, Rock Island–Moline, Moline–East Moline, Moline–Bettendorf). Two are between jurisdictions across the Mississippi from each other, while the other three are intrastate. Among these five relationships there are 101 agreements. If the border plays no role then 40 would be expected among the contiguous parties across the border, while 61 would be found intrastate.

Table 6 clearly demonstrates that the border is an important differentiator, even among contiguous jurisdictions.[18]

TABLE 6

EXPECTED AND ACTUAL DISTRIBUTION OF INTERSTATE AND
INTRASTATE INTERJURISDICTIONAL AGREEMENTS AMONG
THE CONTIGUOUS LARGE CITIES IN THE QUAD-CITY AREA

	Interstate	Intrastate
Expected	40	61
Observed	29	72
		N = 101

One difficulty with this analysis is that it is not apparent how much of the difference between the interstate and intrastate agreements is the result of the legal boundary, and how much of it is because of the physical obstacle of the Mississippi River. Of course, most interstate metropolitan areas are split by a river boundary, so in practical terms the inability to differentiate the impact of these two types of borders may not be too serious.

18. There are no contiguous interstate relations possible between big cities and small jurisdictions or between small jurisdictions and other small jurisdictions. The bridge connecting points are all between large cities, except the new Interstate 80 bridge, which is out in the country.

But this inability does have important theoretical consequences.

Scrutiny of the subject matter of the agreements suggests that both the river break and the legal break have independent impact. Interjurisdictional consulting agreements concerning zoning decisions along city boundaries, for example, are found between some contiguous cities in the Quad-City area. With the wide Mississippi River separating some cities, the planning and zoning officials probably do not worry as much about noncontiguous land use across the river. A single bridge connects Moline with Bettendorf, and two connect Davenport with Rock Island. But many roads intersect adjoining jurisdictions on the same side of the river—and occasionally a road is the actual boundary, presenting still another series of problems potentially amenable to interjurisdictional solution. So the river itself probably accounts for part of the pattern of agreements. On the other hand, when Rock Island, Moline, and East Moline joined together to create the metropolitan airport, there was no legal authority for Davenport or any other Iowa jurisdiction to join in. If Davenport had been in Illinois, it is not certain that this city would have joined the other three in the venture, but it seems like a reasonable possibility. So the river and the state boundary probably play independent parts in explaining the relatively fewer interjurisdictional agreements between the two states. This survey has not isolated or measured the different impact of these two factors.

There is one important way in which it is unfortunate that there is no more precise measure of the different impact of the river and the state line upon extensiveness of agreements. If the river itself could be shown as the major differentiator, the fewer interjurisdictional agreements which occur might be viewed as the simple result of the jurisdictions having fewer activities with spillover effects—hence less need for cooperative efforts. The river could serve as a good fence. On the other hand, if the legal boundary is the major differentiator, perhaps interjurisdictional agreements are less flexible and useful solutions to spillover interstate service problems than they are to intrastate service problems. The Quad-City data do not clearly support either of these interpretations, unfortunately.

The Mississippi River border has been depicted as a variable related to fewer interjurisdictional agreements. But perhaps the more notable finding is the permeability of this barrier. While agreements are less frequent across this line, they are still very frequent. Such agreements occur between contiguous parties and between noncontiguous ones. They occur between big cities and other big cities, big cities and small, and a limited number occur among the small jurisdictions.

Interjurisdictional agreements in the Quad-City area are sufficiently flexible instruments, so they are frequently employed even across state lines. The impact of the state jurisdiction as a barrier to agreements remains cloudy. It is certainly not an absolute or near absolute barrier, as much of the literature would indicate. Independently, the state line may not even be a very important barrier at all. In the Quad-Cities the Mississippi River as a break may account for a large part of the pattern of agreements, rather than the legal boundary.

IMPORTANCE OF INTERJURISDICTIONAL AGREEMENTS

While agreements are extensive, this fact is not evidence that they are important in impact. Does the extensive network of interjurisdictional agreements actually deal with major problems facing this metropolitan polity? Does this form of integration amount to any real coordination of effort among these jurisdictions? This is a crucial, although difficult and ambiguous question. To handle this question even briefly, it becomes necessary to assign some ranking to the different "problems" associated with urban and metropolitan areas, and then to compare this list with the subjects covered in the interjurisdictional agreements. Further, if the subjects dealt with prove to be important, do the interjurisdictional agreements provide much of a solution, or are they just peripheral and minor in their impact?

While interpretations like this are exceedingly difficult and ambiguous, it is clear that most prior observers have thought that interjurisdictional agreements did not deal with important questions in very important ways. Because of these assertions an effort will be made to discuss the subject matter of agreements, although analysis of the content of contacts will be avoided in reporting many of the other processes of integration.

While it is necessary to examine the question of subject matter upon the basis of valuations which lack any intuitive order, and qualitative judgments, some of the arguments against major impact concern the supposed forms of the agreements. This seems to have a more precisely measurable aspect. Bollens and Schmandt indicate that one of the limiting characteristics of interjurisdictional agreements is that many of them are standby mutual aid agreements. "They are operative only when certain conditions come into existence and they remain in operation only so long as these conditions are present."[19]

It is reasonable to argue that "only" in emergencies is just when cities need cooperative effort the most. But, in accepting the above interpretation of mutual aid agreements, in the Quad-City area most of the agreements are not of an emergency standby nature. Out of the 252 agreements,

19. Bollens and Schmandt, The Metropolis, p. 377.

58 can be called standby mutual aid agreements. This amounts to a sub-stantial number, but the greatest number of agreements are not in this category. Nor are all of these agreements strictly reciprocal, as Bollens and Schmandt also assert is necessary,[20] and most other observers assume. Among the mutual aid agreements are 21 between big cities and small jurisdictions. Very few of these are "reciprocal" in the sense that there is a balance of give and take between the jurisdictions. In most instances, the large cities have equipment and professional personnel and the small jurisdictions do not. "Mutual aid" is a misnomer. The large cities can and do assist the small jurisdictions, with only token, if any, recompense. The small jurisdictions are shy of resources to respond to requests for aid from their putative part-ners. Agreements are found which are between partners with unequal re-sources, in which one partner is the major beneficiary. Quid pro quo and strict reciprocity are not always the approach of these agreements. They take some other forms in the Quad-City area. Some of the perceived limita-tions to significant agreements between jurisdictions in metropolitan areas do not seem to be compelling in the Quad-City area.

An evaluation of the *importance* of the different subjects of interjuris-dictional agreements, as contrasted to their *forms*, depends upon judg-ments, rather than counts. Appendix B provides the code by which the subjects were recorded, and the frequency of each of these types of agree-ments. The reader is invited to test the assertions below against this list—although he will be restricted by the coding classification system which was used.

In the Quad-City area, agreements concerning maintenance of public law and order are very frequent among all types of jurisdictions. They cover such police agreements as exchanging arrest information, police radio tie-ups, a coordinated road block system, police patrolling agreements in border areas, and a frequently employed system of mutual aid agreements. A series of standby agreements between the human rights boards would also fit in this category. Maintaining law and order seems to rank high on most peo-ple's lists of problems of the modern American metropolis. The agreements within existence would seem to provide a major means of coordinating the police work in the Quad-Cities.

A large number of agreements concern interlibrary service, but this prob-ably does not rank very high on most people's list of metropolitan problems.

Transportation agreements of various kinds abound. Most students of metropolitan problems count transportation as a major concern. Undoubt-edly many of these agreements deal with rather technical matters—main-taining border roads, patrolling a bridge, etc. On the other hand, the joint

20. Bollens and Schmandt, *The Metropolis*, p. 378.

operation of a metropolitan airport is fairly crucial. Agreements concerning integrated snow removal operations can become rather important when large winter storms hit.

Planning agreements now provide for a very substantial integration of planning and zoning activities for the whole Quad-City area. A number of health agreements exist—although many public health problems are not yet subjects of interjurisdictional agreements. Sewage disposal agreements are also found. Park and recreation agreements exist, covering a number of different program areas. As previously indicated, there even exists a mutual aid agreement among the human rights people. It is hard to evaluate the significance of this last agreement. Some insiders report that the human rights groups operated as a type of intelligence system in the summer of 1966, to the extent of giving timely warning of the arrival in the Quad-Cities of "troublemakers" from Chicago (or St. Louis, depending on the source) who were bent on creating a riot. Such is remotely possible.

In any event, it seems that interjurisdictional agreements deal with many subjects which are widely conceived to be of major importance in American metropolitan areas. Less major topics are also common. For the major subjects covered many of the agreements provide mechanisms which the author judges to be of some importance. Other agreements are surely peripheral to solutions to metropolitan problems.

In the Quad-City area the conclusion is that interjurisdictional agreements deal with a wide variety of subjects. Many deal with major concerns for metropolitan areas. These agreements provide for regularized cooperative efforts in solving not only a substantial *number* of issues, but this number includes some of the major issue areas facing the American metropolis.

4

Direct Official Communication

Intergovernmental personal exchanges among Quad-City officials which occur in the course of work by means of meetings, telephone conversations, mail correspondence, and other interpersonal transactions deserve close scrutiny. An extensive examination is warranted for several reasons. For one thing, many students believe that such interpersonal exchanges are the substance of the whole academic interest in "intergovernmental relations" as a field of study. Students of "metropolitan politics" have also been concerned with such dealings. Perhaps as a consequence of these developed interests, there are many asserted (but largely untested) propositions in the literature upon these types of relationships. Many of these propositions are subject to systematic testing in this chapter.

Another reason for extensive coverage of the interpersonal exchanges in the course of work is that it seems patent that this is a very important potential integrative mechanism. While no effort is made to ordinally classify the potential processes of integration which are examined in this study, it is intuitively clear that direct communications in the course of work are very important (to the extent that they exist). When dealing with the other direct interpersonal transaction measures which have been gathered in this study, it becomes necessary to assert (often on the basis of authority), or assume, that if public officials have dealings with each other through professional associations, clubs, etc., this is promoting integrative action among the cities. Even without "authority" these assumptions and assertions are reasonable, but no such problem is encountered when dealing with interpersonal transactions in the course of work. The categorical definition indicates that these types of transactions are concerned with the political activities of the jurisdictions.

The first important question is simply the extensiveness of the *incidence* of interjurisdictional contact in the course of work of these elected and appointed public officials. The characterizations of local intergovernmental activity as *ad hoc* and sporadic by many of the students of metropolitan politics, would suggest that the incidence of intergovernmental contact in the course of work would be quite low—but no handy measure exists as to what is "quite low." A review of the separate literature on "intergovernmental relations" would probably raise the expectation concerning extensiveness of intergovernmental personal contact among public officials.

The Siouxland study provides one useful comparative statistic. Of the 63 administrative level officials in Sioux City, 53 had personal dealings with other area governments (84.1 per cent) in the course of their work.[1] Some important differences exist between the Siouxland study and this one. Sioux City is a central city of a small metropolitan area; the other local governments in that study included counties (including the one in which Sioux City is located, so that many relationships were statutorily decreed); the survey included all administrative level officials, not just department heads and heads of boards and commissions; it did not include the mayor or council. Nonetheless this is a good comparative statistic, for by any estimate available from the literature, the Sioux City officials were very extensively engaged in interpersonal dealings with the other area governments. The Siouxland Study provides evidence that extensive relationships in the Quad-City area are not simply attributable to some special conditions which exist in the area.

All 227 respondents were asked whether they personally had any phone calls, face-to-face meetings or mail correspondence in the course of their work with local officials from any of the other nine municipalities within the last year. One hundred and eighty-six, or 81.9 per cent had personal dealings in the course of their work with officials from other Quad-City jurisdictions. These very extensive contacts are the result of consistently high reports of communication in the course of work from each of the ten jurisdictions. In Milan all the officials had contact in the course of their work. Hampton has the smallest per cent of their public officials reporting contact, but even here seven of eleven respondents (63.6 per cent) engage in this type of activity.

Werner Landecker suggests that the per cent of persons in a total group network who are isolated is a good negative index of communicative integration.[2] On that basis the Quad-City officials constitute an absolute level of very high communicative integration. Personal direct communication in the course of work among the Quad-City officials is a very extensively used process in accounting for the maintenance of this plural political community.

1. H. Paul Friesema, *Communications, Coordination, and Control Among Local Governments in the Siouxland: A Study of Intergovernmental Relations* (Iowa City: Institute of Public Affairs, University of Iowa, 1965).
2. Werner S. Landecker, "Types of Integration and Their Measurement," reprinted in Paul F. Lazarsfeld and Morris Rosenberg, eds., *The Language of Social Research* (New York: Free Press of Glencoe, 1965), pp. 23–25.

TABLE 7

Jurisdiction	Total Number of Officials With Contact in Course of Work	Number of Officials	Per Cent of Officials With Contact in Course of Work
Davenport	31	35	88.6
Rock Island	30	36	83.3
Moline	30	38	79.0
East Moline	22	27	81.5
Bettendorf	16	22	72.7
Silvis	16	19	84.2
Milan	14	14	100.0
Carbon Cliff	13	15	86.7
Hampton	7	11	63.6
Riverdale	7	10	70.0
	186	227	81.9

Jurisdictional variation in the extensiveness of communication in the course of work is quite small. When the ten jurisdictions are classified on the basis of size, it is apparent that largeness or smallness of the jurisdictions does not account for any variation in this measure. In the five large cities 129 out of the 158 (81.7 per cent) respondents report contact. In the five smaller jurisdictions, 57 out of 69 (82.6 per cent) report contact. Thus the distribution is almost identical.

Nor does the particular state in which the jurisdictions are situated have any measureable impact on extensiveness of contact. Fifty-four out of the 67 Iowa respondents, or 80.6 per cent, are engaged in intergovernmental contact in the course of their work. One hundred thirty-two out of 160, or 82.5 per cent of the Illinois respondents report this contact.

Extensiveness of communication in the course of the public duties of the Quad-City officials is consistently high among the ten jurisdictions. No city's officials are insulated from contact with their neighbors. Little variation in incidence is found among the individual cities or between the big jurisdictions and the small ones. The state in which the cities are located is also an unimportant differentiation. Not only is this particular process extensively used in the Quad-Cities, but its use extends generally, and almost equally, to all jurisdictions.

In engaging in this type of contact, the public officials could have dealings with from one to nine other Quad-City jurisdictions. Table 8 presents the number of jurisdictions with which the 186 Quad-City officials with dealings have contact in the course of their work.

TABLE 8

NUMBER AND PER CENT OF OTHER QUAD-CITY JURISDICTIONS WITH WHICH
PUBLIC OFFICIALS HAVE DEALT IN THE COURSE OF WORK
(N = 186 OFFICIALS WHO HAVE CONTACT)

Number of Other Jurisdictions	Total of Those With Contact Indicating Contact With This Many Other Jurisdictions	Per Cent of Those With Contact Having Contact With This Many Other Jurisdictions
One other	40	21.5
Two other	23	12.4
Three other	22	12.1
Four other	27	14.5
Five other	29	15.6
Six other	13	7.0
Seven other	27	14.5
Eight other	3	1.6
Nine other	2	1.1
Total	186	100.0

It can be seen in this table that the scope of the contacts varies substantially. Out of 186 officials who report intergovernmental communication, 40 have dealings with only one other Quad-City jurisdiction (21.5 per cent). But some 146 officials (78.5 per cent) have dealings with more than a single other Quad-City jurisdiction. One hundred twenty-three (66.1 per cent) of those with contact have dealings with more than two other jurisdictions. Thus the scope of relationships is also high (considerably more than half of *all* respondents have contact in the course of their work with more than two other Quad-City jurisdictions). It is true, at the other end of the table, that only two officials themselves have had dealings in the course of work with all other nine jurisdictions. But this table clearly demonstrates that many of the respondents have dealings with many of their neighboring jurisdictions. The spread of relationships is not limited to sociometric partnerships.

The contacts of the public officials may be between one official and another (*bilateral*), among officials from more than two Quad-City municipalities (*multilateral—Quad-City*) or among Quad-City municipalities, but including other non-Quad-City jurisdictions (*multilateral—other*). Table 9 presents the distribution of these different settings of exchange. (Multilateral contact occurs very largely in one type of exchange—face-to-face meetings.)

TABLE 9

COMPARISON OF SETTINGS OF INTERPERSONAL EXCHANGE USED
BY QUAD-CITY OFFICIALS ENGAGED IN INTERPERSONAL
COMMUNICATION IN THE COURSE OF WORK

Setting of Exchange	Number of Officials With Contact Who Use This Setting	Per Cent of Those With Contact Who Use This Setting
Bilateral	175	95.6
Multilateral—Quad-City Officials	92	49.7
Multilateral—including non-Quad-City Officials	49	26.5
Number of officials having contact in course of work = 185		

Bilateral relations are most extensive. Only 4 per cent of all officials having contact in the course of work do not engage in some bilateral exchanges. Almost half of the respondents with contact have interjurisdictional dealings in multilateral settings involving only Quad-City municipalities. Slightly over a quarter also report contact which involved governments outside the ten-jurisdiction Quad-City system.

One standard description of local intergovernmental activity within metropolitan areas is that relations are on an *ad hoc* basis. While different and occasionally confused meanings are attached to this description, an adequate refutation of all such interpretations would occur if it could be demonstrated that interjurisdictional relationships are not only extensive, frequent, and systematic, but that the contacts deal with subjects which are related and recur over time. It has already been demonstrated that in the Quad-City area interpersonal exchanges in the course of work are very extensive. Throughout this chapter the systematic nature of the contacts is outlined.

All the respondents who acknowledged contact with officials from any of the other Quad-City municipalities were asked: "In previous years have you or your office had contact with (*that municipal government*) on the same or similar types of subjects?" This was asked for each issue the respondent had listed. Table 10 presents the responses. Close to 90 per cent of the reported relationships involved issues which recurred over other years. The topics of these exchanges did not occur once and then disappear. From the Quad-City data it appears that characterizations of local intergovernmental activity within metropolitan areas as being *ad hoc* does not provide an adequate interpretation. There appears to be persistence and structure in the relationships.[3]

TABLE 10

NUMBER AND PER CENT OF PERSONAL CONTACT IN COURSE OF WORK
WHICH HAS INVOLVED ISSUES WHICH HAVE RECURRED, AND
WHICH HAVE NOT RECURRED IN OTHER YEARS

Recurrence of Issues	Total	Per Cent
Some issues recurring	175	87.0
Not recurring	10	13.0
	185	100.0

One important and related question about the contacts which has yet to be dealt with concerns their *frequency*. For each relationship indicated by the Quad-City officials, they were asked about how frequently they had been in contact with the other jurisdictions within the last year. Table 11 reports the responses which were checked. More than 80 per cent of the relations occurred more than once; 60 per cent occurred more often than twice within the last year.[4]

TABLE 11

FREQUENCY OF PERSONAL CONTACT IN THE COURSE
OF WORK IN THE LAST YEAR $(N = 709)$

Frequency	Total	Per Cent
Only once	128	18.1
Upon two occasions	150	21.2
Six or fewer occasions	194	27.4
Twelve or fewer occasions	115	16.2
More often than this	122	17.2
Total	709	100.0

3. In my Siouxland study the responses to an open-ended question about subjects of communication were coded into categories of subjects dealing with special "one-shot" projects, recurring matters, and both. Out of 192 sociometric relationships, 168 (87.5 per cent) involved subjects that were recurring matters, or that included both recurring and special "one-shot" projects.
4. In the Siouxland study exactly comparable data is not available. There the respondents were asked frequency in terms of once a week, month, quarter, year, or less often than this. About 60 per cent of the responses indicated contact at least on a quarterly basis.

The general pattern of interpersonal relationships seems clear for the Quad-City area. Intergovernmental contact in the course of work is very extensive throughout the metropolitan area. Relations are frequent as well as extensive. The subjects of contact are heavily weighted towards issues which recur over other years, in which the same type of relationships existed. These data are remarkably consistent with the findings about the interjurisdictional activity of the officials in the Sioux City area. The standard interpretation that local intergovernmental relations are *ad hoc* and sporadic is not found to be adequate for the Quad-Cities. There is pattern and persistence to the personal interjurisdictional activities.

It is usually assumed that the intergovernmental relations of cities within metropolitan areas are carried on in a *quid pro quo*, or reciprocal basis. A bargaining model is usually expected. This perceived system is often considered to hinder the solution of problems, for activity supposedly will occur only in the instance in which some type of even bargain can be struck.

The analysis of interjurisdictional agreements in chapter three indicated that many of those exchanges could not be categorized as *quid pro quo*, reciprocal relationships. It is important to inquire whether interpersonal exchanges are limited to reciprocal relationships. The differential resources within the control of the separate jurisdictions initially called into question the interpretation that interjurisdictional agreements were reciprocal. In a similar manner, the different levels of professional expertise and political skills from jurisdiction to jurisdiction (and even department to department) raises the question of how reciprocal the interpersonal relations could be. For whose benefit are these exchanges? Table 12 presents the answers of the Quad-City officials. The respondents were asked to select how many of five options described the beneficiaries of their contact with each city with which they had personal contact. For each option between a third and a half of the choices were selected. Over a third indicate that some of their dealings concern problems of primary concern to their own government. Exactly the same number of responses indicated some dealings which concerned problems which were primarily of concern to the other government. About half of the dealings included items which affected both governments about the same. The reverse of this is probably of most interest. Half of the dealings were assessed as not including issues which affected both jurisdictions about the same. It is still quite possible, of course, that over the long run, the benefits of contact even out. This year's dealings may be assessed as primarily for one party's benefit, but next year the other party may feel free to call on the government official he helped the year before. Some evidence on this long-term reciprocity can be inferred from the patterns of the beneficiaries of contact when these are analyzed separately between the individual cities. That analysis is postponed until later in the chapter. At this juncture it seems clear, simply from observing the marginals, that a strictly reciprocal, *quid pro quo* system is not in operation. A substantial number of contacts concern problems of primary interest to only one of the parties, with the other jurisdiction presumably offering advice or assistance. A substantial number of dealings are also seen as simply transmitting information, not about any specific problem. More than 45 per cent of the relationships involved problems or issues which were seen as affecting the area as a whole, and not simply the two governments involved in the exchange.

TABLE 12

PUBLIC OFFICIALS' ESTIMATES OF BENEFICIARIES
OF CONTACT IN THE COURSE OF WORK

Estimates of Beneficiary of Contact	Number Estimating Any Contact With the Beneficiary	Per Cent*
Primarily problem for your own government	254	35.7
Primarily problem for the partner	254	35.7
Affect both about the same	353	49.7
Transmit information—not about specific problem	308	43.3
Problem affecting whole area	324	45.6

* N = 711. While 724 contacts in the course of work relationships were reputed, only 711 usable responses to this question were reported.

Even assuming that benefits will even out in the long run, the review of the data suggests rather forcefully that quite an easy system of personal interjurisdictional contact is found in the Quad-City area. This would seem quite reasonable, when it is recalled how extensive and frequent is the contact. This very extensiveness and frequency of contact probably insures a system of easy exchange, in which calculations of jurisdictional benefit are submerged to a willingness to help a neighboring jurisdiction (or friend) solve a problem. Interpersonal accommodations have been established and worked out.

One explanation for the easy system of interpersonal exchange which has been advanced in the literature is that the functional specialists of the different jurisdictions have much in common, including a shared normative view, professional respect, and common interests. Many reporters have asserted that a very large segment of all intergovernmental activity (not only within metropolitan areas, but throughout the American federal system) is the result of professional and functional counterparts having frequent contact.[5] It is even suggested that the extent of interjurisdictional activity which occurs along "functional" lines is having a profound effect upon the internal organization of the separate jurisdictions.[6]

The widely asserted proposition that interjurisdictional activity is heavily weighted toward contact among functionally equivalent officials can be explored with the Quad-City data. All respondents selected from a prepared list the specific departmental officials with whom they had dealings within the preceding year. These responses were subsequently coded into categories in which dealings were with counterparts only, elected noncounterparts only, appointed noncounterparts only, and the combination of these possibilities. The coding was generous toward finding counterpart contact. Thus, for example, a planning engineer having contact with both a city engineer and a planner in another jurisdiction was listed as having counterpart contact with each. But it should be borne in mind that even when generously coded, equivalent positions are frequently not found. In some instances counterpart contact is impossible. If the Municipal Art Gallery Director of Davenport has any interjurisdictional contact, it must be with noncounterparts, for there are no other municipal art directors. This classification scheme includes the mayors and councilmen as counterpart categories. While much of the literature deals with administrative, as distinguished from political officials, the same question seems important with respect to the elected officials—and of course noncounterpart exchanges may occur between administrators and other mayors or other councilmen.

Out of 724 paired relationships for which data is available, 297 (41.0 per cent) are only between counterparts. Almost 60 per cent of the relationships with cities involved the respondents in dealings with officials from those cities who were *not* their functional, political, or professional equivalents. Thus another standard assertion must be modified when applied to the Quad-City area. While "functional" contacts are extensive (535 of the 724 paired relationships, 73.9 per cent, involved *some* contact with functional counterparts), they are not nearly the only types of contact which occur. More than a quarter of the reported exchanges did not involve dealing with a functional counterpart at all. A majority of these noncounterpart exchanges were between appointed officials on the one hand and elected officials on the other.

The reason for this somewhat surprising finding is not altogether clear. One important element in the explanation may be that these municipal

5. Morton Grodzins, *The American System*, ed. Daniel J. Elazar (Chicago: Rand, McNally & Co., 1966).
6. H. Paul Friesema, "Some Organizational Implications of Intergovernmental Activity Within Metropolitan Areas," *Midwest Review of Public Administration* 1 (February 1967), 11–16.

bureaucratic structures are still relatively undifferentiated, compared with other types of organizations. Weberian ideals about clear divisions of labor may be of a less-compelling nature in these local government units. If this is the case, actual program responsibilities may be diffused throughout the municipal government. Contact with bureaucratic functional counterparts may not be the sum total of intergovernmental exchange because the common classifications of jobs may hide large differences in informal responsibilities of public officials. If this is true, the widely asserted but more general hypothesis that intergovernmental programs (of all kinds) are fostering the functional organization of governments may need more testing.

TABLE 13

PERSONAL CONTACT IN COURSE OF WORK WITH COUNTERPARTS, ELECTED
NONCOUNTERPARTS, AND APPOINTED NONCOUNTERPARTS
IN THE QUAD-CITY AREA

Officials Contacted	Number With This Contact	Per Cent
Counterparts only in all dealings	297	41.0
Elected noncounterparts only in all dealings	117	16.2
Appointed noncounterparts only in all dealings	46	6.4
Counterpart and elected noncounterpart in all dealings	91	12.6
Counterparts and appointed noncounterparts in all dealings	42	5.8
Elected and appointed noncounterparts	26	3.6
Counterparts elected and appointed noncounterparts	105	14.5
	724	100.0

Another factual assertion which is frequently found in the literature about intergovernmental activity is that the dealings in metropolitan areas, such as they are, consist essentially of administrative contacts, rather than exchanges between politicians. This is often explained as the result of the presumed or asserted fact that administrators have a more cosmopolitan orientation, whereas the politicians tend to be quite locality centered in their values. It is occasionally even suggested that interjurisdictional activities within metropolitan areas are most successful and common if they are rather surreptitiously carried out by the administrators (i.e., hidden from the politicians and the public). Even when a factual assertion is not made that intergovernmental contact equals administrative contact, many other studies presume that contact is an administrative activity, simply by not studying the interjurisdictional activities of the elected officials.

The Quad-City study allows for the examination of this reasonable proposition as it applies to the area. While other dimensions of politician vs. administrator orientations will be examined elsewhere in this study, here the simple factual question of the comparative interjurisdictional activities of the different types of public officials will be explored. Table 14 presents a comparison of the interjurisdictional activities in the course of work of the mayors, the councilmen, and the other public officials in the Quad-Cities.

TABLE 14

INCIDENCE AND SCOPE OF INTERJURISDICTIONAL ACTIVITIES OF MAYORS, COUNCILMEN, AND OTHER QUAD-CITY OFFICIALS

Officials	Incidence of Contact in Course of Work	Total Number of Officials	Per Cent of Officials With Contact	Mean Number of Jurisdictions Officials Have Had Contact With
Mayors	10	10	100.0	7.3
Councilmen	54	69	79.3	2.9
Others	122	148	82.4	3.0
	186	227		

The elected officials (mayors and councilmen) have about the same amount of incidence of interjurisdictional contact (81.0 per cent) as the other officials (82.4 per cent). While the per cent with contact is very similar, the 100 per cent level of activity of the mayors is particularly notable.

The *scope* of interjurisdictional activity is also noteworthy. The elected officials have a mean contact level with 3.4 other jurisdictions, while the other officials average dealings with three jurisdictions. While the councilmen and the other officials have very similar *scopes*, once again the mayors' activity stands out. They *average* dealings with more than seven of the nine other jurisdictions.

The assertion and assumption that interjurisdictional dealings are essentially between administrative officials is not found to be true in the Quad-Cities. The mayors and councilmen are very extensively involved in interjurisdictional activity in the course of their public duties. The mayors evidence an extremely high level of activity, even when compared with the high level of activity of the other officials.

The explanation for the heavy involvement of the elected officials, and particularly the mayors, in intergovernmental activity may be accounted for because of the longer and more extensive experience of the elected officials in the Quad-City area. While many of the appointed officials may be hired from outside the metropolitan area, and may have their whole work experience in the area limited to employment by a single municipal government, the elected officials may be more likely to have personal experience in other area jurisdictions. Contrary to many suppositions, it seems possible that elected officials, and particularly the mayors, are characteristically the "metropolitans" (if not "cosmopolitans") of the Quad-City political community, when compared with the orientations and activities of the department heads and heads of boards and commissions. The supposed shared values and interests of functional counterparts from different jurisdictions may be matched or exceeded by the prior experiences of the elected officials in the metropolitan area. This point is speculative, for the data are not available, but, if true, it is of some importance for understanding the operation of metropolitan political systems.

The personal exchanges among the public officials in the Quad-Cities have been found to be very extensive and widespread throughout the area. They involve recurring issues and problems. The communication which occurs in the course of work is very frequent. An easy system of contact exists, in which calculations of mutually equivalent advantage have not been the sole basis for exchange. Interjurisdictional activity within the Quad-Cities is not confined or even heavily loaded upon exchanges between the functional counterparts within the separate jurisdictions. Nor are these exchanges the sole province of the administrators, for the elected mayors and councilmen are highly involved in this type of activity. The mayors score particularly high in the measurement of their interjurisdictional activities. Every one of these findings is different than could be anticipated from reviewing the literature. Like the interjurisdictional agreements, discussed in Chapter 3, interjurisdictional communication in the course of work is found to be much greater than anticipated. This activity also explains a great deal of the political integration which is achieved in the Quad-City political community.

Observers have frequently argued that because intergovernmental contacts were voluntary, they could not provide an adequate mechanism for coordinating activities within metropolitan areas. The contrary position (espoused by many officials themselves) is not argued here. But what is asserted is that interjurisdictional contacts, at least in the Quad-Cities, are of quite a different nature than they are usually pictured. They do provide a well-used mechanism for coordinating activities within this area. From the Quad-City study, it is possible to suggest that many of the standard interpretations about metropolitan political structure rest upon presumptions of fact which are untenable.

In addition to uncovering the many facets of personal interjurisdictional communication which occur in the course of the public work of the Quad-City officials, it is important to explore the particular pattern of the relationships which exist in the area. As in Chapter 3, one primary interest will be in exploring the extensiveness of relations which are big city to big city, big city to small jurisdiction, and small jurisdiction to small jurisdiction. A subissue will be to explore the satellite-sun type of relationships between large cities and the immediately adjacent small jurisdictions. A second major interest will be to examine interstate and intrastate contact. The effect of contiguity upon contact will be examined also.

In Chapter 3 the state of previous research and speculation was such that derivative hypotheses could be stated and tested. That happy state does not occur in the present analysis, and there is little reason to expect any particular pattern to be found.

A very difficult methodological problem must be faced when trying to measure the comparative strength of the different interjurisdictional bilateral relationships. This arises because the reported relationships flow in two ways. For example, Davenport officials report on their personal contact with Rock Island, and Rock Island officials report on their dealings with Davenport. These two reports do not necessarily match. Many city officials in one city may have dealings with a single official in the other, or some officials may have contact with a person in another jurisdiction who was not even interviewed (an assistant department head, or an ex-official, for example). On the other hand some of the reported activities are undoubtedly matched up. An official in Davenport and an official in Rock Island may each report an exchange between the two, but only one exchange occurred, and it must not be counted as two.

This problem has been resolved by taking as the basic measure of relationship the report of any contact in the course of work of the public officials. The strength of the relationship between any two jurisdictions is then the per cent of their combined officials who have had contact with each other in the last year. Thus 23 of the 35 Davenport officials (65.7 per cent) reported contact with Rock Island. Eighteen of the 36 Rock Island officials (50.0 per cent) reported contact with Davenport. These figures were combined so that 41 of the 71 officials of the two cities reported being engaged in contact in the course of work. This amounts to 57.8 per cent. This percentage measure is the essential measure of the strength of the relationship between Davenport and Rock Island. It can be compared with similar measures for each other of the 45 bilateral relationships. For example, nine of the 35 Davenport officials reported contact with Riverdale, while four of the ten Riverdale officials have had dealings with Davenport. Thirteen of 45 officials have contact (28.9 per cent). This relationship is roughly half as strong as the one between Davenport and Rock Island. A total of 2,043 relationships were possible (227 respondents, each potentially having contact with nine other jurisdictions). Data was gathered on 2,034 of the possible relationships (one respondent did not answer this sequence). Of the 2,034 possible combinations, 724 actually were reported to occur (35.6 per cent).

The first question arising concerns the extent to which the relations between jurisdictions are confined among the big cities, are between big cities and small jurisdictions, and are among the small jurisdictions. Davenport, Rock Island, Moline, East Moline, and Bettendorf are classified as the large cities, and the other five are referred to as small jurisdictions. Table 15 reports the pattern of big city to big city, big city to small jurisdiction, and small jurisdiction to small jurisdiction relationships. The five large cities, among themselves, double the percentage of participation over what occurs between the large cities and the small jurisdictions. Among themselves the small jurisdictions have even a smaller per cent participation.

TABLE 15

DISTIBUTION OF PERSONAL CONTACT IN THE COURSE OF
WORK AMONG DIFFERENT SIZED JURISDICTIONS IN THE QUAD-CITY AREA

Type of Relationship	Number Occurring	Possible Occurrences	Per Cent of Possible Occurrences Which Occur
Big city–big city	350	632	55.4
Big city–small municipality	311	1125	27.6
Small municipality–small municipality	63	227	22.7
	724	2034	35.6

This pattern is quite similar to the pattern of interjurisdictional agreements (Chapter 3), where the agreements among the large cities were just over twice as common as ones between the big cities and small jurisdictions. The pattern of interpersonal communication among the small jurisdictions is somewhat altered from the interjurisdictional agreement pattern. While still in third place, stronger interpersonal relationships do exist among the small jurisdictions, when compared to the relations between the small jurisdictions and the large cities. Another evidence of strength of relationship comes from using the standard sociometry indicator of assessing the favored others for each particular jurisdiction or groups of jurisdictions. Table 16 presents the first four sociometric choices for each municipality, as determined by the per cent of their public officials who indicate that they have had contact in the course of work within the past year. Out of 20 choices possible, the officials from the five large cities indicated 17 large city "others," and only three small jurisdiction "others." Fifteen of the 20 small jurisdiction choices are with large cities, while only five are with other small jurisdictions. Thus the large cities are preoccupied largely with each other. The small jurisdictions are largely preoccupied with the large cities, with much less involvement with the other small jurisdictions.

These results are also cumulative to the pattern established in Chapter 3.

TABLE 16

FIRST FOUR SOCIOMETRIC "CHOICES" UPON BASIS OF PERSONAL
CONTACT IN COURSE OF WORK FOR EACH JURISDICTION
IN THE QUAD-CITY AREA

Jurisdiction	First Four Sociometric "Choices"
Davenport	Bettendorf, Rock Island, Moline, East Moline
Rock Island	Moline, Milan, East Moline, Davenport
Moline	Rock Island, East Moline, Silvis, Davenport
East Moline	Silvis, Moline, Rock Island, Davenport
Bettendorf	Davenport, Rock Island, Moline, East Moline
Silvis	East Moline, Carbon Cliff, Moline, Rock Island
Milan	Rock Island, Moline, Silvis, East Moline
Carbon Cliff	Silvis, Moline, East Moline, Rock Island
Hampton	East Moline, Carbon Cliff, Silvis, Rock Island
Riverdale	Bettendorf, Davenport, (Rock Island, Moline, East Moline) (tie)

Grouped Sociometric "Choices" Among Different Sized Jurisdictions Within the Quad-City Area			
Type of Relationship	Number Occurring	Possible Occurrences	Per Cent Which Occur
Big city–big city	17	20	85.0
Big city–small jurisdiction	3	20	15.0
Small jurisdiction–big city	15	20	75.0
Small jurisdiction–small jurisdiction	5	20	25.0

There interjurisdictional agreements between the large cities and small jurisdictions were found to involve a relatively small amount of the resources of the large cities, but were heavily relied upon by the small jurisdictions. This cumulative pattern suggests some interesting possible interpretations. For one thing, a general feeling has prevailed among students of metropolitan politics (and the frequently articulate central city mayors) that the small suburban jurisdictions were relatively unresponsible parts of the metropolitan polity. This may be so, depending on what criteria of responsibility is advanced. But this cumulative evidence of the patterns of transactions which is found in the Quad-City area indicates that the small jurisdictions are more oriented toward the large cities than the reverse, and in some ways more vulnerable to the actions of the large cities.

The pattern of interjurisdictional personal communication evidences the very extensive relations which are possible among larger jurisdictions. When added to the prior transaction measure, this suggests that large jurisdictions which find themselves in close time-space proximity to each other are and will be able to develop and maintain close direct relations with each other.

The pattern of big city–small jurisdiction and small jurisdiction–small jurisdiction relationships also suggests that it is rather difficult for small jurisdictions to join together and "gang up" on the larger cities, despite the wide coverage of some incidence of this type of alliance. Upon the basis of the transaction measures so far explored in the Quad-City area, the small jurisdictions have close and separate ties to the larger cities, and relatively few ties to each other. That is the political infrastructure upon which the particular political issues of the day are played out. There is not a strong pre-existing network of ties among the small jurisdictions to facilitate an alliance over an issue, at least with the measures considered thus far.

While it has been seen that the large jurisdictions do not reciprocate either the comparative importance attached to interjurisdictional agreements or the interpersonal preoccupation which the small jurisdictions expend in their relations, it will also be recalled that many of the interjurisdictional agreements which exist between big cities and small jurisdictions were not quid pro quo agreements. In many cases, the large cities provide assistance without getting anywhere near equivalent return. It is important to see if this pattern is also the same in the interpersonal relations between large cities and small jurisdictions.

In the first section of this chapter the beneficiaries of the interpersonal contacts were explored. Many were found to benefit one but not both parties to the exchange. If these responses are examined to see what the assessments of benefits are between the big cities and small jurisdictions, many more are seen as primarily of benefit to the small jurisdictions than are seen as of primary benefit to the large cities. One hundred eighty-six relationships are reported between the two types of municipalities in which benefits of the exchange are primarily for one of the partners. One hundred and eighteen of these, or 63.4 per cent, are assessed as being primarily of benefit to the small jurisdiction. Thus the benefits do not even out between the big cities and small jurisdictions. The small jurisdictions receive more than they give. The pattern of the prior chapter is repeated once again.[7]

In the analysis of interjurisdictional agreements, a type of satellite-to-sun pattern was discussed, concerning the special nature of the relations between some of the small jurisdictions and their immediately neighboring large city. When the four satellite-sun combinations are explored for the strength of interpersonal contacts, it is found to be a strong relationship.[8] Ninety-seven out of 150 possible contacts are reported (64.7 per cent). This compares with 214 out of 975, or 22.0 per cent for other large city to small jurisdiction relationships. Thus relations between satellite-sun municipalities are about three times as strong as other relations between small jurisdictions and the large cities.

The satellite-sun pattern might reflect a broader pattern of strong relations between contiguous municipalities, regardless of size. Table 17 compares the strength of contiguous and of noncontiguous relations. Contiguous relations are found to be very much stronger than noncontiguous ones.[9] Interjurisdictional agreements were found to be about two and one-half times more frequent than could be expected if agreements were evenly distributed. Contiguous interpersonal contacts are not that much stronger than the general distribution (35.6 per cent of all possible combinations), but they are better than twice as common as noncontiguous ones. Much of the satellite-sun type of relations can be explained as part of a common pattern of strong ties between contiguous jurisdictions.

7. The above data reflect the assessments of both large city and small jurisdiction respondents as to who benefits. This could conceivably vary quite a bit. For example, the large city officials might well assess themselves as primarily dispensors of favors, but the small jurisdiction officials might have quite a different perspective. In fact, this does not occur. Big city officials estimate that 65.1 per cent of their one-way benefited contacts are primarily to benefit the small jurisdictions (54 of 83). Small jurisdiction officials estimate that 62.1 per cent (64 of 103) of their one-way benefited dealings with large cities were largely for their own benefit. Thus both groups of officials estimate that the big cities provide assistance to the small jurisdictions much more frequently than it is returned, and furthermore the proportions are very close.
8. The four satellite-sun relations are Rock Island–Milan, East Moline–Silvis, East Moline–Hampton, and Bettendorf–Riverdale.
9. "Contiguity" is coded as occurring on an interstate basis only if the jurisdictions are directly linked by bridges. Thus, Davenport is contiguous to Rock Island, and Bettendorf to Moline.

TABLE 17

DISTRIBUTION OF PERSONAL CONTACT IN THE COURSE OF WORK AMONG
CONTIGUOUS AND NONCONTIGUOUS JURISDICTIONS
IN THE QUAD-CITY AREA

Type of Relationship	Number Occurring	Possible Occurrences	Per Cent Which Occur
Contiguous	328	527	62.2
Noncontiguous	396	1507	26.3

The impact of the Mississippi River state border upon interpersonal contact in the course of work of the public officials can be seen in Table 18.

TABLE 18

DISTRIBUTION OF INTERSTATE AND INTRASTATE CONTACT IN THE
COURSE OF WORK IN THE QUAD-CITY AREA

Type of Relationship	Number Occurring	Possible Occurrences	Per Cent Which Occur
Interstate	267	940	28.4
Intrastate	457	1094	41.8

Interstate relations are not as strong as intrastate ones. Once again the variance from the total distribution of contact is considerably less than the comparable distribution of interjurisdictional agreements across state lines.[10]

The interpretation of the impact of contiguity and of the state border involves one problem which also arose in the last chapter. It is not altogether clear whether the lower level of contact among noncontiguous jurisdictions, or ones in different states, is attributable to some barrier to contact which exists, or is the simple result of there being fewer reasons for these officials to come in contact with each other. What is clear is that contiguous contact is more common than noncontiguous contact, and intrastate contact is more common than interstate contact. But the level of interpersonal contact in both of these areas is less affected by these ecological variables than were the interjurisdictional agreements. Contiguity and the

10. The same pattern appears when the interjurisdictional contact among the large cities is compared for interstate-intrastate variation. Some 47.7 per cent (178 out of 373) interstate contacts are reported, while 66.4 per cent of the intrastate ones are found (172 of 259). The total distribution among the large cities, it will be recalled, is 55.4 per cent.

state border still make a difference, but not as substantial a one. There is a high level of noncontiguous contact, and a high level of contact across the state border.

The existence of a high level of contact among noncontiguous and interstate partners, even though less than among contiguous and intrastate partners, suggests that the lower comparative strength of the former relationships may not reflect any barrier function to contact, but may be simply the result of there being less cause for these officials to come in contact with each other. The fact that phone calls among the jurisdictions are all "local," and that it is occasionally faster for a city official to drive to a noncontiguous city hall than to a contiguous one (i.e., East Moline to Carbon Cliff is much faster than East Moline to Moline), also suggests this.

The remarkable consistency of the patterns of interpersonal contact with the patterns of interjurisdictional agreements is worth special emphasis. All patterns of interjurisdictional agreements are also found to exist with the personal contacts in the course of work among public officials. The findings are cumulative.

Interjurisdictional personal contact in the course of work is found to be very widespread in the Quad-City area. It amounts to an extensively used process for integrating the activities of the separate jurisdictions. Much of the maintenance of the political community occurs because the public officials deal with each other in regular, recurring, and systematic fashion. The large cities have very extensive dealings with each other, and somewhat less with the smaller jurisdictions. The small jurisdictions, in turn, are oriented toward the larger cities, and not toward each other. A satellite-sun system of exchange has been detected. The large cities are seen to be providing assistance out of proportion to what they receive from the smaller jurisdictions. Contact among contiguous jurisdictions is more frequent than among noncontiguous jurisdictions, and intrastate contact is stronger than interstate contact. In all of these findings clearly established patterns of exchange are uncovered. The Quad-City metropolitan area is found to have much political structure. Its relationships do not constitute an "overgrown jungle," "hodge-podge," "morass" or any of the other epithets suggesting an unfathomably complex system now being hurled about by political scientists who despair at finding the system or structure for metropolitan areas.

5

Other Direct Processes of Political Integration

The balance of the direct channels of exchange among the Quad-City jurisdictions remain to be examined. These potential processes of direct contact
among the public officials are through the municipal and professional associations, social organizations, political parties, business associations, and personal friendships which occur. Each of these processes, to the extent that it
is active, may supplement the other integrative mechanisms in accounting
for the continued maintenance of the plural political community.

PROFESSIONAL AND MUNICIPAL ASSOCIATIONS

The integrative role of professional and governmental associations in
cementing the American federal system together has been stressed by many
scholars. The impact of such associational exchanges within metropolitan
areas is not yet as clear as it is with respect to federal-state-local associations,
or the associations of functional specialists generally. To the extent that
such associations promote national programs and shape values of officials
generally, they should do the same within the metropolitan context. This
may even occur within metropolitan or other local areas in which there are
no members of such associations, simply by virtue of the national impact of
the interest articulation and value-shaping functions of these associations.
The extent to which these types of associations also provide a mechanism
for direct exchanges among metropolitan area officials is an important question. The Quad-City officials were asked about their participation in any
such organizations. They were asked to identify officials from the other
Quad-City jurisdictions with whom they actually came in contact, and
to estimate the frequency of such contact. The questions were asked to
include not only the narrowly professional interest associations (an inspectors association, for example), but also any general municipal associations in

which the respondents had actually participated (a municipal league, for instance). The responses to this sequence of questions provide the basis for an analysis of this process of personal direct exchange among the Quad-City municipalities.

Quad-City officials belong to professional and general municipal associations in large numbers. Out of 227 officials, 162 report participation in at least one such association in which they report contact with officials from other Quad-City municipalities.[1] Table 19 presents the participation reported by the officials from the separate jurisdictions.

TABLE 19

CONTACT WITH OTHER QUAD-CITY OFFICIALS THROUGH MUNICIPAL AND
PROFESSIONAL ASSOCIATIONS FOR OFFICIALS OF EACH JURISDICTION

Jurisdiction	Officials With Contact	Total Number of Officials	Per Cent of Officials With Contact
Davenport	23	35	65.7
Rock Island	27	36	75.0
Moline	29	38	76.3
East Moline	21	27	77.8
Bettendorf	18	22	81.8
Silvis	15	19	79.0
Milan	13	14	92.9
Carbon Cliff	6	15	40.0
Hampton	6	11	54.4
Riverdale	4	10	40.0
Total	162	227	71.4

The range of reported contact is from about 93 per cent down to 40 per cent. Thus each individual jurisdiction has a sizable proportion of public officials engaged in this type of interjurisdictional exchange. Illinois officials are slightly greater joiners of these organizations than are Iowa officials (73.1 per cent of Illinois officials report this type of contact, compared to 67.2 per cent of the Iowa officials). The five larger jurisdictions have a little higher proportion of their officials engaged in professional and municipal associations (74.7 per cent of the large city officials, compared to 63.8 per cent of the small municipality officials). The high proportion of small juris-

1. Note that this does not include membership in an association through which, to the respondent's knowledge, he had no direct contact with officials in other Quad-City jurisdictions. Thus, for example, the interviewers turned up more than one local member of some professional type associations without local chapters, in which the joint memberships did not result in any metropolitan contact. Such memberships are not included in this analysis.

diction participants in this type of exchange is worth emphasis. It could be expected that the full-time professionals and skilled politicians of the large cities would be joiners of professional and municipal associations. This could not be anticipated for the small jurisdictions.

The frequency with which the Quad-City officials have contact with the other cities is presented in Table 20. It is apparent that most of these memberships are not only on paper. By and large, the officials engaged in such organizational activity have contact on a reasonably frequent basis with officials from other jurisdictions. More than 60 per cent (494 of 801) of the bilateral exchanges occurred more than once within the previous year; over a quarter of them occurred more than six times.

TABLE 20

FREQUENCY OF CONTACT WITH OFFICIALS FROM OTHER
QUAD-CITY JURISDICTIONS THROUGH MUNICIPAL
AND PROFESSIONAL ASSOCIATIONS

Frequency	Number of Contacts	Per Cent of Contacts
None within last year	138	17.2
Only once	169	21.1
Upon two occasions	107	13.4
Six or fewer occasions	185	23.1
Twelve or fewer occasions	164	20.5
More often than this	38	4.7
Total	801	100.0

One other important issue concerns who are the participants in this type of exchange. Table 21 compares the reported participation of mayors, councilmen, and the other city officials.

TABLE 21

INCIDENCE OF INTERJURISDICTIONAL CONTACT THROUGH
MUNICIPAL AND PROFESSIONAL ASSOCIATION OF
MAYORS, COUNCILMEN, AND OTHER
QUAD-CITY OFFICIALS

Officials	Incidence of Contact	Number of Officials	Per Cent With Contact
Mayors	9	10	90.0
Councilmen	47	69	68.1
Others	106	148	71.6
	162	227	71.4

Such exchanges are not limited to the department heads or other functionally interested officials. The number of elected officials engaging in this type of exchange (70.9 per cent) is very close to the per cent of other city officials (71.6). Again, the mayors' activities stand out. This finding seems particularly interesting in conjuction with the data on exchanges between functionally equivalent and nonequivalent officials in the course of work, reported in Chapter 4. Not only are contacts in the course of work not confined within the professional specialties, but the elected officials are as involved in associational exchanges as the department heads. Taken together, these findings suggest that the argument that intergovernmental activity is strongly promoting functional autonomy within municipal bureaucracies needs further examination. Within the Quad-City area, a very large segment of two important processes of intergovernmental exchange are not confined to narrow functional or professional exchanges. While no data was recorded upon the scope or frequency of participation in any one particular organization, it is clear that participation in municipal league activity far superseded activity within any of the other municipal or professional organizations. These organizations (League of Iowa Municipalities; Iowa Large Cities Group; Illinois Municipal League, and Northwest Illinois Municipal League) garnered participation from all categories of officials, and from every jurisdiction (but because of the state border, not all together). Other organizational meeting grounds included an inspectors association, a mayors association, police and fire groups, bar associations, health societies, safety councils, municipal finance officers association, public works groups, waterworks groups, human rights groups, associations of librarians, and many more.[2] These municipal and professional associations provide a setting for exchange among the Quad-City officials which is used extensively. They provide a substantial mechanism or process for integrating the activities of the separate jurisdictions. Exchanges are widespread and frequent, and they occur among all levels of officials.

The patterns of exchange through municipal and professional associations are examined first to compare the big city–big city, big city–small jurisdiction, and small jurisdiction–small jurisdiction contacts. (See Table 22.) The strength of relationship is once again measured by the per cent of officials from each of the forty-five bilateral combinations who have contact with each other through municipal and professional associations.

Contact among the large cities is substantially stronger than the other patterns. In absolute terms it is quite high, with over half of all the possible

2. A joint East Moline–Silvis Municipal Employees Credit Union was included as a professional group, although it is obviously a hybrid type of organization. While officials from both cities belonged, few reported direct contact with each other this way.

combinations actually occurring. This is another facet of the extensive relationships possible among large cities in close proximity to each other.

TABLE 22

DISTRIBUTION OF CONTACT THROUGH MUNICIPAL AND PROFESSIONAL
ASSOCIATIONS AMONG DIFFERENT SIZED JURISDICTIONS
WITHIN THE QUAD-CITY AREA

Type of Relationship	Number of Contacts Which Occur	Number of Possible Occurrences	Per Cent of Possible Occurrences Which Occur
Big city–big city	324	632	51.3
Big city–small municipality	394	1135	34.8
Small municipality–small municipality	82	277	29.7
Total	801	2043	39.2

Once again there is a somewhat stronger relationship between the big cities and the small jurisdictions than among the small jurisdictions themselves. Even with municipal and professional association exchanges the five small jurisdictions have stronger ties with the five large cities than with each other.

A satellite-sun pattern exists which is parallel to other patterns of satellite-sun exchanges. Fifty-six per cent of the possible combinations between large cities and immediately adjacent small municipalities occur (93/166), compared to 34.8 per cent of the other contacts between large and small jurisdictions.

The satellite-sun type of exchanges are part of a consistent pattern of strong ties between contiguous jurisdictions, irrespective of the size of the municipalities. This pattern is the same as found in earlier measures. Table 23 compares the exchanges which occur through municipal and professional associations by contiguous and noncontiguous jurisdictions.

The strength of contiguity is not as great for municipal and professional exchanges as it was for contact in the course of work, but it is still very strong. It is hard to explain this strong relationship. While many of the municipal or professional associations are organized on some sort of area basis, with the exception of the state border, no basis seems to exist to explain why officials from contiguous jurisdictions would have so much more contact than the noncontiguous ones. Perhaps part of the explanation lies in the *other* patterns of exchange between contiguous jurisdictions.

TABLE 23

DISTRIBUTION OF CONTACT THROUGH MUNICIPAL AND PROFESSIONAL
ASSOCIATIONS AMONG CONTIGUOUS AND NONCONTIGUOUS
JURISDICTIONS IN THE QUAD-CITY AREA

Type of Relationship	Number of Contacts Which Occur	Number of Possible Occurrences	Per Cent of Possible Occurrences Which Occur
Contiguous	304	527	57.7
Noncontiguous	497	1507	33.0
Total	801	2034	

Because of these exchanges the officials may already know each other, and consequently may have associational contact which impressed itself in their memory. It is obviously quite possible that people from still other Quad-City jurisdictions attend some of the meetings of these associations, but their presence is not known or remembered by the respondents. Such potential meetings would probably be eufunctional in promoting political integration through a process of direct exchange (although it could still promote integration by shaping values).

The impact of the Mississippi River border upon associational contact is clear from Table 24. Intrastate exchanges are substantially more than twice the strength of the interstate exchanges. But the interstate contact through municipal and professional associations is still quite high. Much of the difference between interstate and intrastate contact is undoubtedly accounted for by the legal state boundary, which is also the boundary for many of these types of organization memberships.

TABLE 24

DISTRIBUTION OF INTERSTATE AND INTRASTATE CONTACT THROUGH
MUNICIPAL AND PROFESSIONAL ASSOCIATIONS
IN THE QUAD-CITY AREA

Type of Relationship	Number of Contacts Which Occur	Number of Possible Occurrences	Per Cent of Possible Occurrences Which Occur
Interstate	225	949	23.7
Intrastate	576	1094	52.7
Total	801	2043	

Personal contact among the Quad-City jurisdictions through participation in municipal and professional associations is extensive and frequent. The patterns are in the same direction as the patterns of interjurisdictional agreements and contact in the course of work. The municipal and professional associations present extensively used forums of exchange which help to maintain the Quad-City political community.

SOCIAL ORGANIZATIONS

The clubs, fraternal groups, and other social organizations may also provide the setting for exchange among the Quad-City public officials. Whether such exchanges directly deal with pressing problems or involve decision-making (as much folklore about what transpires at city clubs and country clubs suggests), or simply provide a forum for friendly exchanges in which the officials come to know each other and each other's problems better, contact will have an impact upon the integration of activities within the metropolitan area.

Many of the clubs and other social organizations in the Quad-Cities are organized on an area-wide basis, and even when organized upon a single jurisdiction basis, members frequently live in a different city than the home jurisdiction of the organization. Given this, plus the expectation that political officials will be frequent joiners of clubs and other social organizations, it is important to enquire into the interjurisdictional exchanges which occur among the Quad-City officials through joint participation in such social organizations.

Ninety-two Quad-City officials, or 42.7 per cent of them, report membership in social organizations in which they have contact with officials from other Quad-City jurisdictions. Thus, social organizations provide a forum of exchange for many public officials. Table 25 presents the distribution of the reports on this type of exchange. The big city officials are just about as likely to engage in this type of exchange as the small jurisdiction officials (41.7 per cent of the big city officials, compared to 44.9 per cent of the small jurisdiction officials). Iowa officials report somewhat more exchanges (49.3 per cent) than do Illinois officials (40.0 per cent).

While many Quad-City officials report contact through social organizations, the per cent is considerably lower than the per cent reporting contact through professional and municipal associations. All of the cities' officials report less social contact than municipal and professional contact, except for Carbon Cliff and Riverdale where officials report a higher level of social contact. For these two jurisdictions in particular, whose officials are least

TABLE 25

Jurisdiction	Incidence of Contact	Total Number of Officials	Per Cent of Officials With Contact
Davenport	19	35	54.3
Rock Island	15	36	41.7
Moline	14	38	36.8
East Moline	10	27	37.0
Bettendorf	8	22	36.4
Silvis	8	19	42.1
Milan	7	14	50.0
Carbon Cliff	8	15	53.3
Hampton	2	11	18.2
Riverdale	6	10	60.0
Total	97	227	42.7

active in professional and municipal associations, contact through social organizations may provide a basic channel of political integration.

The frequency with which the Quad-City officials with social organization contact actually meet the officials from other jurisdictions is reported in Table 26. Less than 10 per cent of the 283 reported bilateral exchanges had not occurred within the last year. Most occurred more than once within the last year. Thus, for many of the Quad-City officials, social organization memberships provide a mechanism for recurring exchanges with officials from other jurisdictions.

TABLE 26

FREQUENCY OF CONTACT WITH OTHER QUAD-CITY OFFICIALS
THROUGH SOCIAL ORGANIZATIONS

Frequency	Number of Contacts	Per Cent of Contacts
None in last year	28	9.9
Only once	94	33.2
Upon two occasions	60	21.2
Six or fewer occasions	60	21.2
Twelve or fewer occasions	34	12.0
More often than this	7	2.5
Total	283	100.0

Table 27 presents the responses of the mayors, councilmen, and other city officials. A smaller per cent of the mayors, so active in other exchanges, have social organization contact than councilmen or other officials. Perhaps most notable is the comparatively high per cent of other officials with this type of conduct. Mayors and councilmen, as elected politicians would be expected to be organization joiners. But the other public officials report nearly as high a per cent of contact through social organizations (41.9 per cent) as the elected officials (44.3 per cent). Compared with the two previous processes of exchange (direct contact in the course of work and through municipal and professional organizations), in which "common sense" indicated that most action would be by the department heads and other nonelected officials, but this did not prove to be so; in this case, the elected politicians were expected to be far more active than they proved to be.

TABLE 27

Officials	Incidence of Contact	Number of Officials	Per Cent With Contact
Mayors	3	10	30.0
Councilmen	32	69	46.4
Others	62	148	41.9
Total	97	227	42.7

The patterns of this type of exchange fall into the familiar form. Of all the possible combinations 283/2,043, or 13.9 per cent, occur. Table 28 presents the combined number and per cent of officials engaged in this type of exchange by big city–big city, big city–small jurisdiction, and small jurisdiction–small jurisdiction. Big city–big city contact more than doubles the big city–small jurisdiction contact, which in turn is a stronger relationship than small jurisdiction–small jurisdiction. Social exchanges follow the same pattern as the previous exchanges. Among the reported contacts between big cities and small jurisdictions a disproportionate segment are between the satellite-sun combinations. Thirty of 166 (18.1 per cent) of these occur, compared to 87 of 969 (9.0 per cent) other big city–small jurisdiction relations. Contiguity generally results in more contact through social organizations. The relationship between contiguous jurisdictions is two and one-half times as strong as between noncontiguous jurisdictions (136/527, for 25.7 per cent of the contiguous relationships; 147/1516, for 9.8 per cent for the noncontiguous relation-

TABLE 28

DISTRIBUTION OF CONTACT THROUGH SOCIAL ORGANIZATIONS
AMONG DIFFERENT SIZED MUNICIPALITIES
WITHIN THE QUAD-CITY AREA

Type of Relationship	Number of Contacts Which Occur	Number of Possible Occurrences	Per Cent of Possible Occurrences Which Occur
Big city–big city	147	632	23.3
Big city–small jurisdiction	117	1135	10.3
Small jurisdiction–small jurisdiction	19	276	6.9
Total	283	2043	

ships). Contact among intrastate jurisdictions is also substantially stronger than interstate contact. One hundred ninety-four of 1,094 possibilities occur among intrastate jurisdictions (17.4 per cent). This compares to a strength of 89/949 (9.4 per cent) for interstate relationships.

The social organizations provide a channel of exchange among the Quad-City jurisdictions which gets substantial use, even if less than the prior two channels of personal contact. These organizational contacts constitute one more network in the maintenance of the plural community. The patterns are essentially the same as with the other personal transaction flows thus far analyzed. Contact continues to be greatest among the large cities, least among the small jurisdictions. Contiguity and the state border are both major differentiators of the flows of exchange. Even though contact is considerably less between noncontiguous jurisdictions and those across the Mississippi River from each other, these are not absolute barriers. A fair number of social organization exchanges occur these ways, as they did with the other processes of integration.

POLITICAL PARTIES

The decentralized American party system results in a great deal of autonomy for the local party organizations. But the local party organizations have at least formal connection to the national and state party organization, and thus to the surrounding local organizations of that party. Moreover, one of the chief concerns and focus of activity for local party organizations, at least where local elections are contested and competitive (as in the Quad-City area) is control of the county offices. Local party organization is essentially based upon county lines, even when city party organizations also exist. For these reasons the city officials who are involved in partisan politics might well have occasion to deal with officials from other munici-palities through joint work in the political parties. Party organizations could provide the setting for many exchanges, which might also help to account for the maintenance of the plural political community.

Many assertions that parties cannot and do not provide much of an inte-grating mechanism for metropolitan areas are found in political science literature. This is often stated to be the case because of a supposed split in partisan attachments between the Democratic-leaning central cities and the Republican suburbs. Recent voting research indicates that this supposed split is more complex than previously believed. As Chapter 2 indicated, this is not the characteristic partisan split in the Quad-City area.

While parties are not thought to provide much of an integrating mech-anism for metropolitan areas, some case studies indicate that upon occasion powerful individuals can make use of party machinery to get or enforce agreement on some course of action from more than one jurisdiction within metropolitan areas. The Quad-City study provides an analysis of the role of the party organizations in integrating this metropolitan area by analyzing the personal exchanges which occur under the auspices of the local branches of the national parties.

Table 29 reports the contacts recalled by the city officials through activi-

TABLE 29

CONTACT WITH OTHER QUAD-CITY OFFICIALS THROUGH JOINT WORK
IN POLITICAL PARTIES FOR OFFICIALS OF EACH JURISDICTION

Jurisdiction	Incidence of Contact	Total Number of Officials	Per Cent of Officials With Contact
Davenport	10	35	28.6
Rock Island	8	36	22.2
Moline	14	38	36.8
East Moline	8	27	29.6
Bettendorf	4	22	18.2
Silvis	6	19	31.6
Milan	3	14	21.4
Carbon Cliff	3	15	20.0
Hampton	2	11	18.2
Riverdale	1	10	10.0
Total	59	227	26.0

ties with either the Democratic or Republican parties. More than a quarter of the Quad-City officials report some contact through the parties with officials in other jurisdictions. While this is much below the other measures, contact through party organization work is far from negligible. Every jurisdiction reports at least one official with this type of contact. For each of the five larger cities, those having this type of contact include Democrats and Republicans, although both parties are not represented among those with contact in some of the smaller jurisdictions. So while some of the large cities are overwhelmingly one party controlled, they have at least some officials with ties to the other party, and through that party to municipal officials in the other jurisdictions.

The per cent of Iowa officials reporting this type of exchange is quite close to the Illinois figure (22.4 per cent of Iowa officials; 27.5 per cent of Illinois officials). Big city respondents report only a slightly greater per cent of this type of exchange than the small jurisdiction officials (27.9 per cent of big city officials; 21.7 per cent of small jurisdiction officials).

The frequency of exchanges which occur through party work is presented in Table 30. One hundred forty-seven of 2,043 of the *possible* relationships actually occur, or 7.2 per cent. More than half of the reported exchanges have recurred more than once within the last year. For those who report this type of exchange, many have almost regular contact with officials in other jurisdictions through their party activities.

TABLE 30

FREQUENCY OF INTERJURISDICTIONAL CONTACT WITH OTHER
QUAD-CITY OFFICIALS THROUGH JOINT WORK
IN POLITICAL PARTIES

Frequency	Number of Contacts	Per Cent of Contacts
None in last year	22	15.0
Only once	30	20.4
Upon two occasions	39	26.5
Six or fewer occasions	38	25.9
Twelve or fewer occasions	13	8.8
More often than this	5	3.4
Total	147	100.0

The mayors and councilmen are far more active in political parties than the other public officials. Six of the ten mayors report contact through their party. Thirty of the 69 councilmen report such contact. Thus 45.6 per cent of the elected officers report contact through party work. This com-

pares with 23/148 for other officials, or 15.5 per cent. This is the first transaction measure in which the common-sense expectation about who would
be the chief actors has turned out to be accurate.

The patterns of exchange through party organizations deviate from the
other exchange patterns. While big city–big city contact is most extensive,
the small jurisdictions have somewhat stronger bonds among themselves
than occurs with the big city to small jurisdiction relationships.

TABLE 31

DISTRIBUTION OF CONTACT THROUGH JOINT WORK IN POLITICAL
PARTY ORGANIZATIONS AMONG DIFFERENT SIZED
JURISDICTIONS WITHIN THE QUAD-CITY AREA

Type of Relationship	Number of Contacts Which Occur	Number of Possible Occurrences	Per Cent of Possible Occurrences Which Occur
Big city–big city	62	632	9.8
Big city–small jurisdiction	63	1135	5.6
Small jurisdiction–small jurisdiction	22	276	8.0
Total	147	2043	

This pattern may be the result of the partisan attachments of the different
jurisdictions (four of the five small jurisdictions tend to be Democratic; four
of the five larger cities tend to be Republican). Whatever the reason, in
absolute terms there still is not very much contact among the small jurisdictions.

Satellite-sun combinations are still substantially stronger than other big
city–small jurisdiction exchanges (23/166, or 13.9 per cent of satellite-sun
possibilities; 40/969, or 4.1 per cent of others). The satellite-sun exchanges
are between jurisdictions sharing partisan leanings on three occasions: East
Moline–Silvis (D); East Moline–Hampton (D); Bettendorf–Riverdale
(R); and not sharing them on one occasion, Rock Island (R)–Milan (D).
Contiguity accounts for 14.8 per cent of the possible relationships (78/527),
compared to a strength of 4.6 per cent for noncontiguous relationships.
These are all in the familiar pattern.

Table 32 presents the comparison of interstate and intrastate transactions
through party organizations. The contact between interstate jurisdictions
through the political parties is miniscule. While interstate contact has been
substantially less than intrastate contact by other measures, this is the first

process in which transactions have come close to not occurring. It seems clear that party organizations do not provide much base for exchanges across the state line. In the Quad-City area, the Mississippi River is almost unbridged, as far as the parties as agents of integration are concerned.

TABLE 32

DISTRIBUTION OF INTERSTATE AND INTRASTATE CONTACT THROUGH
JOINT WORK IN POLITICAL PARTIES IN THE QUAD-CITY AREA

Type of Relationship	Number of Contacts Which Occur	Number of Possible Occurrences	Per Cent of Possible Occurrences Which Occur
Interstate	19	949	2.0
Intrastate	128	1094	11.7
Total	147	2043	

Generally the party organizations provide a reduced channel for personal exchange. But the number and per cent of exchanges are still sufficient so that they add another layer to the overlapping connections between the public officials of the Quad-City jurisdictions.

BUSINESS ASSOCIATIONS

Many of the Quad-City officials have business interests in addition to their municipal positions. Most all of the elected officials depend on a nonpolitical income. Many of the other officials, especially in the small jurisdictions, work at a nongovernmental occupation in addition to their public responsibilities.

These businesses and jobs may bring the public officials into contact with one another. If public officials from different jurisdictions have business or work associations with each other, another aspect of the political structure of the metropolitan community is indicated. The transactions which occur between business associates, clients, colleagues, or co-workers who are officials of the different jurisdictions may be important in explaining political integration in the Quad-Cities.

Seventy-one of the Quad-City officials report that they have work or business connected contact with people who are officials for other Quad-City jurisdictions. This amounts to a remarkably high 31.3 per cent of all the municipal officials. Table 33 presents the number and per cent of officials from each of the Quad-City jurisdictions who indicate that they have business or work dealings with officials from other Quad-City jurisdictions. All jurisdictions have a sizable number of officials who report this contact. The small jurisdictions have a much higher per cent with contact (44.9 per cent) than the larger jurisdictions (25.3 per cent). This surely reflects the higher number of part-time officials in the small jurisdictions. Iowa officials and Illinois officials are evenly balanced in their reported contact (34.3 per cent, Iowa; 30.0 per cent, Illinois).

Three mayors, 28 councilmen, and 40 other officials report contact through their private occupation. Thus the part-time elected public officials have a higher level of business exchanges (39.2 per cent) than do the other officials (27.0 per cent), a great many of whom are full-time government officials.

TABLE 33

CONTACT WITH OTHER QUAD-CITY OFFICIALS THROUGH BUSINESS AND WORK ASSOCIATIONS FOR OFFICIALS OF EACH JURISDICTION

Jurisdiction	Incidence of Contact	Total Number of Officials	Per Cent of Officials With Contact
Davenport	9	35	25.7
Rock Island	9	36	25.0
Moline	6	38	15.8
East Moline	7	27	25.9
Bettendorf	9	22	40.9
Silvis	10	19	52.6
Milan	6	14	42.9
Carbon Cliff	5	15	33.3
Hampton	5	11	45.5
Riverdale	5	10	50.0
Total	71	227	31.3

Table 34 compares big city–big city, big city–small jurisdiction, and small jurisdiction–small jurisdiction contact. One hundred ninety-seven of the 2,043 combinations possible do occur (9.6 per cent). Once again big city–big city contacts are stronger, although not by much. Big city–small jurisdiction contacts and small jurisdiction–small jurisdiction contacts have nearly identical strengths. Business and work exchanges seem to occur more evenly among the different sized jurisdictions than did other exchanges.

Satellite-sun contacts continue to be strong (32/166, or 19.3 per cent), when compared to the other exchanges between big and small municipalities (6.8 per cent). But generally, the contiguous business relations are

TABLE 34

DISTRIBUTION OF CONTACT THROUGH BUSINESS AND WORK
ASSOCIATIONS AMONG DIFFERENT SIZED JURISDICTIONS
WITHIN THE QUAD-CITY AREA

Type of Relationship	Number of Contacts Which Occur	Number of Possible Occurrences	Per Cent of Possible Occurrences Which Occur
Big city–big city	75	632	11.9
Big city–small jurisdiction	98	1135	8.6
Small jurisdiction–small jurisdiction	24	276	8.7
Total	197	2043	9.6

better than twice as strong as the noncontiguous ones (contiguous, 16.5 per cent; noncontiguous, 7.3 per cent).

The state boundary again poses a barrier, but not as substantial a one as it was for political party exchanges. Fifty-six of 949 (5.9 per cent) of the possible interstate relations occur, compared to 141/1,094 (12.9 per cent) of the possible intrastate combinations.

The existence, and particularly the extent of business and nongovernmental work connected contact among the Quad-City officials is largely an unexpected dimension of the area's political structure. The sequence of questions was included in an effort to be exhaustive, but without the expectation of anything like the responses which were reported. Apparently the public officials in the metropolitan area often travel in the same economic circles. This probably is important in shaping shared values. It certainly indicates another channel by which many of the Quad-City officials deal with each other. The extensiveness of contact indicates that the business and work associations of the Quad-City officials constitute another important integrative device for maintaining the Quad-City political community.

Personal Friendships

The final measure of personal exhcange among the Quad-City officials is their personal friendships. To the extent that these officials are personal friends with officials from the other jurisdictions, also facilitates the integration of activities between jurisdictions.

All the Quad-City officials were asked, "In addition to any contact you've already listed (all the prior measures), are there people working in any of these Quad-City area local governments who you consider to be close personal friends?" One hundred and four of the 227 respondents (45.8 per cent) reported that they did have close personal friends attached to other Quad-City governments. The number and per cent of officials in each jurisdiction reporting personal friendships is reported in Table 35.

TABLE 35

CLOSE PERSONAL FRIENDSHIPS WITH OTHER QUAD-CITY OFFICIALS
FOR OFFICIALS OF EACH JURISDICTION

Jurisdiction	Incidence of Personal Friendships	Total Number of Officials	Per Cent With Personal Friends
Davenport	16	35	45.7
Rock Island	14	36	38.9
Moline	12	38	31.6
East Moline	14	27	51.8
Bettendorf	10	22	45.5
Silvis	12	19	63.2
Milan	7	14	50.0
Carbon Cliff	9	15	60.0
Hampton	4	11	36.4
Riverdale	6	10	60.0
Total	104	227	45.8

Once again no jurisdiction comes close to being isolated. The range is quite narrow (36.4–63.2). The small jurisdictions report a substantially higher per cent with personal friendships (55.1 per cent) than are reported in the large cities (41.8 per cent). The state variation is unsubstantial (47.7 per cent in Iowa; 45.0 per cent in Illinois), as it has been with every other transaction measure.

Of all the possible combinations, 300 of 2,043 (14.7 per cent) were reported to occur. Despite the higher per cent of small jurisdiction officials reporting personal friendships, the big city to big city combinations continue to be stronger than the other two (Table 36).

The other two relationships are about equal in strength, with small municipality exchanges among themselves being slightly stronger than the relations between the big and small municipalities. The satellite-sun combinations (49/166, or 29.2 per cent) are three and one-half times stronger than other big city-small combinations (74/969, or 7.8 per cent). The contiguous relationships (158/527, or 30.0 per cent) are just about three times as strong as the noncontiguous ones (142/1,507, or 9.4 per cent).

TABLE 36

DISTRIBUTION OF CLOSE PERSONAL FRIENDSHIPS AMONG DIFFERENT
SIZED JURISDICTIONS WITHIN THE QUAD-CITY AREA

Type of Relationship	Number of Reported Personal Friendships	Number of Possible Friendship Patterns	Per Cent of Possible Occurrences Which Occur
Big city–big city	146	632	23.1
Big city–small jurisdiction	123	1135	10.8
Small jurisdiction–small jurisdiction	31	276	11.2
Total	300	2043	14.7

The state border has an impact upon personal friendship patterns, as it has had upon the other personal transactions. Ninety-two (of 949) interstate friendship patterns were reported, compared to 208/1,094 friendship patterns of an intrastate variety. Thus 9.7 per cent of the possible interstate exchanges do occur, while 19.0 per cent of the possible intrastate ones exist. The Mississippi border makes a difference, but many personal friendships still occur among officials on opposite sides of the river.

Personal friendships are another dimension of the web of transactions which exist in the Quad-City area. The reported close friendships of so many Quad-City officials with officials from other jurisdictions is another part of the structure of political activity. These friendship patterns explain, in part, the ability of the separate jurisdictions to maintain a plural community of governments.

MEASURES OF PERSONAL EXCHANGE

The six measures of personal interjurisdictional transactions present a range of strengths. Table 37 compares the per cent of officials indicating exchanges for each of the six measures. It also presents the per cent of possible bilateral contacts which actually occur for each of these processes of integration.

Each process of personal exchange occurs to a very substantial level. Exchanges through political parties, by both measures the least used process, still involve more than a quarter of the 227 respondents. The highest per cent of officials report being engaged in contact in the course of work,

TABLE 37

COMPARISON OF SIX MEASURES OF PERSONAL INTERJURISDICTIONAL
EXCHANGES BY PERCENTAGE OF QUAD-CITY OFFICIALS INVOLVED
AND BY THE PERCENTAGE OF POSSIBLE EXCHANGES
WHICH ACTUALLY OCCUR

Type of Contact	Per Cent Reporting Type of Contact	Rank Order of Reported Contacts	Per Cent of Possible Contacts Which Occur	Rank Order of Possible Contacts Which Occur
Course of work	81.9	1	35.6	2
Municipal and professional organizations	71.4	2	39.2	1
Social organizations	42.7	4	13.9	4
Political parties	26.0	6	7.2	6
Business and work associations	31.3	5	9.6	5
Personal friendships	45.8	3	14.7	3

followed by contact through municipal and professional organizations. But membership in municipal and professional organizations involves the officials in contact with a larger number of other Quad-City jurisdictions than do the exchanges in the course of work. Thus contact through municipal and professional organizations results in the highest per cent of the total possible exchanges. These two processes, which are probably the most overtly or manifestly integrative of the personal exchange measures, are major reasons why the plural political community continues to function without serious problems caused by the separate authority of the individual jurisdictions. Personal friendships among Quad-City officials, contact through social organizations, and the business and work association of many of these officials are other elements of the network of governmental communication within the area. The political parties are the least used mechanism of personal exchange found in the Quad-City area, even though the stereotype of central city Democrats and suburban Republicans is not found. The parties do not provide as much of a coordinating mechanism as the other processes. They still involve 26 per cent of the officials in exchanges, however. The different measures of personal exchange indicate that there is a highly-developed metropolitan political structure involving overlapping patterns of recurring exchanges among the public officials.

The patterns of exchange are not only extensive, but they are quite similar to each other. Table 38 presents a comparison of the big city–big city, big city–small municipality, and small municipality–small munici-

TABLE 38

COMPARISON OF SIX MEASURES OF PERSONAL INTERJURISDICTIONAL
EXCHANGE AMONG DIFFERENT SIZED JURISDICTIONS
WITHIN THE QUAD-CITY AREA

PER CENT OF POSSIBLE CONTACTS WHICH ACTUALLY OCCUR

Type of Contact	Big city– big city	Big city– small jurisdiction	Small jurisdiction– small jurisdiction
Course of work	55.4	27.6	22.7
Municipal and professional organizations	51.3	34.8	29.6
Social organizations	23.3	10.3	6.9
Political parties	9.8	5.6	8.0
Business and work associations	11.9	8.6	8.7
Personal friendships	23.1	10.8	11.2

pality exchanges. By all measures the big city–big city exchanges are the
most extensive. Big city–small municipality contact exceeds small municipality–small municipality exchanges for three processes: contact in the
course of work, municipal and professional organizations, and social organization exchanges. The reverse order is found for the least extensively used
process, political parties. The small jurisdiction–small jurisdiction strength
is greater than big city–small jurisdiction contact on business and work
associations and personal friendships, although these two are virtually equal.
The mean of the six measures is 29.1 per cent for exchanges among the big
cities, 16.3 per cent for big city–small jurisdiction exchanges, and 14.5 per
cent for exchanges among the small jurisdictions. The relative closeness of
the percentages of the latter two hides a big difference in the absolute level
of contact. The contact among small jurisdictions averages 40 officials being
involved per measure, compared with an average 175 officials engaged in
exchanges between big cities and small jurisdictions. Thus the big cities,
among themselves, evidence the highest level of communicative integration, the big city–small municipality combinations the next highest, and
the small municipality–small municipality combinations the lowest. The
small jurisdictions do not give evidence of any alliance structure aimed
at the big cities or anyone else. They have closer ties to the big cities than
they do to the other small jurisdictions. With every measure of personal
exchange, the relations between the four satellite-sun combinations are substantially stronger than other relationships between big cities and small
municipalities. The satellite-sun relations have a mean strength 2.8 times

as strong as the other big city–small municipality relations. Satellite-sun relations are comparatively strongest with personal friendships (3.8) and political parties (3.4), and least strong, comparatively, with municipal and professional contact (1.8).

With every process of personal exchange the contiguous jurisdictions have stronger relations than the noncontiguous ones. The contiguous jurisdictions have a mean strength of 2.6 times as strong as noncontiguous ones. As with satellite-sun patterns, contiguity is most important with respect to personal friendships (3.2) and political parties (3.2), and least important for municipal and professional contact (1.8). The satellite-sun relations are mostly just one type of contiguous relationship. The same pattern appears among the other contiguous jurisdictions, regardless of the size of those jurisdictions.

The Mississippi River state border results in substantially fewer exchanges than among jurisdictions within the same state for each process. Intrastate relations average better than two and one-half times as strong as the interstate relations. The barrier the border puts in the way of political party contact (intrastate are 5.9 as strong as interstate party exchanges) distorts this, for with all other measures intrastate relationships are less than twice as strong as the interstate combinations.

The patterns of personal exchange are remarkably consistent from one process of communication to another, even though the extensiveness of the use of the six processes varies rather widely. The transaction flows are thus patterned in the same way from one transaction to another. Together, they are evidence of extensive networks of exchange involving consistent patterns.

JURISDICTIONAL VARIATION

The patterns of interpersonal exchange which have ben examined have been between different groups of jurisdictions. These group exchanges involve an extremely high correlation among the six processes. The alteration in rank order between big city–small municipality exchanges and small municipality–small municipality exchanges is the only deviation from perfect rank order correlation among the processes of exchange for each pattern which has been examined.

It is important to examine whether this high group correlation corresponds to a high correlation among the individual jurisdictions. When the rank order for the six processes of interpersonal exchange are compared for both the ten separate jurisdictions and for the forty-five bilateral combinations, no different results appear. Table 39 presents the rank order among the ten jurisdictions on the extensiveness of their reported participation in each of the six processes of exchange. The Kendall Coefficient of Concordance (W) for the six measures is a quite low .289. Thus the jurisdictions which are high on one process are frequently low on another. By comparing the rankings of the six processes for each jurisdiction, it can be seen that the town of Silvis has the most extensive mean exchanges, followed by Milan, while Hampton appears to be the least integrated by these personal exchange measures. It is difficult to explain these jurisdictional variations. Hampton is a small jurisdiction, only contiguous to one other Quad-City jurisdiction, but that also describes Milan. Moline, a large city adjoining three other large cities, is ninth ranked of the ten jurisdictions. Even though no clear reason seems to exist for this distribution, it is important to note that a rather wide range of mean rank orders occur among the jurisdictions, and that the correlation among the six measures is quite low.

The forty-five sociometric relationships were also rank ordered for the six processes of interpersonal exchange. Here the Kendall Coefficient of Concordance (W) for the six measures is a quite high .777. The particular bilateral partnerships high on one transaction measures are quite likely to be high on other measures. The five particular combinations which have the *highest* average rates of exchange are all between contiguous intrastate jurisdictions (Davenport–Bettendorf, East Moline–Silvis, Silvis–Carbon Cliff, Moline–East Moline, and Rock Island–Moline). The five combinations with the *lowest* mean rates of personal exchange are all between noncontiguous interstate combinations (Bettendorf–Hampton, East Moline–Riverdale, Silvis–Riverdale, Carbon Cliff–Riverdale, and Hampton–Riverdale). These polar scores are entirely predictable on the basis of the earlier analysis. None needs any special accounting as a deviate bilateral exchange pattern.

While the variation in rank order of the separate jurisdictions is quite extensive, from process to process, the forty-five particular sociometric partners have a high correlation among the six processes. The individual sociometric relations are accounted for by the prior analysis which indicated that strong relationships would occur among contiguous intrastate jurisdictions, while weak relationships would occur among noncontiguous interstate jurisdictions.

CONCLUSION

The processes of interpersonal exchange have been found to be in exten-

TABLE 39

RANK ORDER AND KENDALL COEFFICIENT OF CONCORDANCE (w) FOR USE
OF SIX MEASURES OF INTERJURISDICTIONAL EXCHANGE
FOR OFFICIALS OF EACH JURISDICTION

RANK ORDER FOR REPORTED CONTACT BY TYPE OF CONTACT

Jurisdiction	Course of Work	Municipal and Professional Organization	Social Organization	Political Parties	Business and Work Associate	Personal Friendships	Total of Ranks by Rows
Davenport	2	7	2	4	8	6	29
Rock Island	5	6	6	5	9	8	39
Moline	7	5	8	1	10	10	41
East Moline	6	4	7	3	7	4	31
Bettendorf	8	2	9	8.5	6	7	40.5
Silvis	4	3	5	2	1	1	16
Milan	1	1	4	6	4	5	21
Carbon Cliff	3	9.5	3	7	5	2.5	30
Hampton	10	8	10	8.5	3	9	48.5
Riverdale	9	9.5	1	10	2	2.5	34

$$w = .289$$

sive use. They help account for the maintenance of the plural political community in the Quad-Cities. The exchanges through municipal and professional organizations and the contact in the course of work of the public officials are the most extensively used processes. The political party organizations are least used. But each examined process is used extensively as an integrative mechanism.

Relations are most extensive and well-developed among the large cities. Contiguity and the state border have a major impact on the extensiveness of relations. But, while fewer, relations among noncontiguous and interstate jurisdictions are also very common.

In all of these findings, it appears that there is a highly-developed, systematic and even predictable metropolitan political structure in the Quad-Cities. These direct processes of exchange, while often not overt, are major although hitherto little-examined mechanisms for explaining political integration in metropolitan areas.

6

Indirect Processes of Political Integration

The direct transaction flows among the Quad-City jurisdictions are not the only processes by which the activities of separate units may be integrated. Some mediation may occur through the good offices of third parties. In such systems of indirect mediation, there need be no direct contact between the jurisdictions or their officials. Secondary systems of integration exist within the Quad-City area, and they provide important contributions toward the maintenance of the plural political community.

Three potentially crucial intermediary systems among separate jurisdictions are personally influential individuals acting in this capacity, interest groups, and the corporations which are involved in the metropolitan area. The metropolis-serving news media and the municipal consultants who provide their services to area governments may also play a role of indirect coordination. The existence of such secondary processes of exchange in the Quad-City area deserve close examination.

INFLUENTIAL INDIVIDUALS

Interest in the ability of nongovernmental people to influence political behavior, particularly at the community level, has been a major preoccupation of political scientists and sociologists, at least since Floyd Hunter's *Community Power Structure*.[1] The searching methodological debate plus the substantive contributions which followed are so well known that they do not require further explication here. More recent contributions have developed approaches which seem to move beyond the "either-or" quality of the "reputational" versus "decision-making" approaches. Some of the recent works attempting to meld techniques include *The Rulers and the*

1. Floyd Hunter, *Community Power Structure: A Study of Decision Makers* (Chapel Hill: University of North Carolina Press, 1953).

Ruled,[2] Men at the Top,[3] and Community Influentials.[4] This Quad-City study of the ability of influential individuals to integrate activities of separate jurisdictions should be viewed as a modest effort along these same lines.

For all the research conducted upon power and influence in communities, there is almost a complete hiatus of depth study of the *interjurisdictional* aspects of political influence. Occasionally, the subject is peripherally touched in decision-making case studies, but there is almost no systematic intelligence upon the ability of influential people to integrate actions of separate political units.[5] Perhaps it is a fair assertion that most students of community influence believe that influence coalesces around some jurisdictional or organizational base, and consequently influential citizens probably do not play much of a role in interjurisdictional metropolitan politics. Matthew Holden, Jr., explicitly states his belief that issue resolution between jurisdictions within metropolitan areas is left to official decision-makers, and nongovernmental political actors stay out.[6] The extent to which this is true in the Quad-City area will be explored in this chapter.

In studying the ability of influential citizens in mediating between jurisdictions in the Quad-City area, the emphasis of the research has been two-fold. First, an effort is made to tap the political *structure*, that is the *recurring patterns* of activity. The approach which has been developed hopefully gets beyond the limitations of case analysis of individual decisional events. It is also meant to get beyond the now obvious difficulty of relying on reputation for influence as an index of actual influence. Second, this effort is not designed to uncover "*the*" power structure of the Quad-Cities. It is more modest in purpose. The aim is simply to see whether influential citizens can and do integrate activities of separate jurisdictions by making demands and otherwise being active in the political life not only of their city of residence (or work), but also in other jurisdictions within the metropolitan area.

The procedure used in this effort has involved a two-step process. The first step is directly out of the "reputational" methodology. A list was com-

2. Robert E. Agger, Daniel Goldrich, and Bert E. Swanson, *The Rulers and the Ruled: Political Power and Impotence in American Communities* (New York: John Wiley & Sons, 1964).

3. Robert Presthus, *Men at the Top: A Study of Community Power* (New York: Oxford University Press, 1964).

4. M. Kent Jennings, *Community Influentials: The Elites of Atlanta* (New York: Free Press of Glencoe, 1964).

5. Probably the most useful cases involving interjurisdictional consequences which have come to my attention are in two classic studies in this genre: Edward Banfield, *Political Influence* (New York: Free Press of Glencoe, 1961); and Roscoe C. Martin et al., *Decisions in Syracuse* (Bloomington: Indiana University Press, 1961).

6. Matthew Holden, Jr., "The Governance of the Metropolis as a Problem in Diplomacy," *Journal of Politics* 26 (August 1964), 628–629.

piled of reputed influential citizens, henceforth labeled *municipal activists.*
This list, totaling 35 for the whole Quad-City area, was gathered separately from each of the ten jurisdictions. The procedure was to ask three of
the principal municipal officials of each jurisdiction to provide a list of
people who were "most active and influential in your own municipality's
affairs." This wording probably meant that the list would not include any
"behind-the-scene dealers" who operated through front men, if such oper-
ators existed. On the other hand, it might very well include some whom
Hunter would label "understructure professionals," whose positions
demand that they be politically active. The list was limited to four citizens
for each of the five large cities, and three citizens for the five small jurisdictions, for a total of 35. This arbitrary number was arrived at simply for convenience. If any larger list had been compiled, it would have been too
unwieldy to handle in the rest of this analysis. The list was agreed upon by
the informant municipal officials, either meeting jointly, or with the interviewers going between the informants. The municipal officials who were
the key informants included in all cases the mayor (in one instance, because
of temporary absence of the mayor, the mayor *pro tem*), the city clerk,
and a third official who varied from jurisdiction to jurisdiction. The third
informant was chosen largely on a convenience basis, but he was supposed
to be a "generalist" in his own municipal responsibilities, whom the interviewers believed to be knowledgeable. With these three key municipal
decision-makers as informants, the result was that they were providing the
interviewers with a list of people whom they judged to have been active and
influential in some large measure upon themselves.

In most instances, the informants did not know for what purpose the list
would be used, and the interviewers did not volunteer this information.
It was the interviewers' opinion, however, that many of the informants
believed that their nominees subsequently would be interviewed also.
While the interviewers did not disabuse the respondents of this apparent
belief, they were careful to avoid suggesting this use or any other use for
these names. In the only instance in which the interviewers were specifically asked for the purpose of the list, the informant (a large city mayor)
was told in detail what the purpose would be. Subsequently many of the
officials, particularly those who became interested in the research project,
did become aware of the purpose of the list. No repercussions have occurred
to this writing.

Once the list of 35 municipal activists was compiled, it was incorporated
into the interview instrument. The names were arranged alphabetically,
without any municipal or other identification, and put upon a card to be
handed to all 227 city officials who were the respondents to this interview
schedule.

The interview schedule asked each respondent a series of five questions about the list of municipal activists. First, "Can you identify who these people are?" Second, "Starting from the top again, have you ever discussed municipal affairs or problems with any of these people?" Third, "Do you know any of these men through clubs or social or professional organizations, or on any other basis than in connection with your work?" Fourth, "In connection with your work as a municipal official, have any of these men called upon you with specific requests for information, advice, assistance, or other help with some issue or problem they were concerned about?" Fifth, "In connection with your work as a municipal official, have you ever called upon any of these men with requests for information, advice, assistance, or other help with some issue or problem you have been concerned with?"

The responses to these questions were recorded separately for each municipal activist. Each respondent's answers as to his relations with the municipal activists were scored on a zero through five scale, corresponding to the number of "yes" responses recorded in the sequence of five questions. This score is the basis for the analysis. Using this procedure involves an assumption of *ordinality* in the scores. This seems like a perfectly reasonable assumption in this case. Any score of *one* is the result of a "yes" answer to the first question about whether the respondent can *identify* the municipal activist. Any score *above one* will necessarily include a "yes" response to this question as well. Any score of *two* will require a "yes" response to *either* question two or three as well as question one. (Neither questions four nor five could be answered "yes" without also answering one and two "yes," for a minimum score of three.) Under this ordinal classification no assumption need be made that any *combination* resulting in a score is equivalent to another combination resulting in the same score. (For example, a score of two, resulting from the 1 + 2 combinations need not be treated as equal to a score of two resulting from the 1 + 3 combinations. The assumption is simply that any score of two is greater than a score of one, and less than a score of three or more.) This ordinal classification results in a scale which reflects varying degrees of activity for the municipal activists. Any score of two or more reflects some activity by a municipal activist vis-à-vis the respondent. Any score of three or more is considered to reflect a significant degree of political involvement by that municipal activist.

The essential question these responses and scores answer is whether or not people who are active and influential within one jurisdiction are also active and influential within other jurisdictions within the Quad-Cities. If these 35 respondents are found to score high in more than their own jurisdiction, it can be asserted that influential individuals can and do play an integrative role within metropolitan areas. On the other hand, if these 35 respondents did not score high interjurisdictionally, more caution must be used in asserting the negative. This researcher does not have enough confidence in the first step selection process of municipal activists to say that if *these* 35 were not influential across jurisdictional lines then, *a fortiori*, no *other* influential people could be. Even people with no *reputation* for action in any separate jurisdiction might play such a role. During the interview period, for example, a minor county official, without apparent influence resources, was able to secure contributions from a number of the jurisdictions for a perhaps quixotic program of traffic safety education for motorcyclists in the Quad-Cities. He played this overt integrative role without being considered "influential" in anyone's book.

As one internal test of the reliability of the selection of municipal activists, a prior decision was made that if any municipal activist did not have a mean score of at least two from the answers of the municipal officials who were the respondents from the same jurisdiction from which he was nominated, he would be eliminated from further analysis. All 35 municipal activists far exceeded what proved to be a low level of acceptance. Thus the first step reputational selection *did* succeed in identifying municipal activists who had been politically active within their own jurisdiction. The succeeding analysis will indicate how active and influential they have been in other jurisdictions.

The municipal activists turn out to be widely known to Quad-City public officials. The average number of Quad-City officials from jurisdictions *other than* the one from which the municipal activists were *nominated*, who can identify each municipal activist is 48.7.[7] Thus close to 50 public officials in other jurisdictions can identify the typical nominated municipal activist. The *range* of identifications was from 135 for an East Moline municipal activist, 131 for a Moline municipal activist, and down to seven for a Bettendorf municipal activist.

The large city municipal activists are more visible than their small jurisdiction counterparts. The mean number of identifications for large city municipal activists is 57.1, whereas the mean number of identifications of small jurisdiction municipal activists is 37.5, or far from negligible.

Table 40 presents the mean number of public officials from other jurisdictions who identify the municipal activists from each jurisdiction. The nominated municipal activists from East Moline, followed by Moline, are

7. All data presented is in terms of numbers rather than percentages. There are a total of 227 respondents, but the relevant number for percentages would be 227 minus the number of respondents from the city from which each municipal activist was nominated.

most widely known. The Silvis nominees are least widely identified. But it is clear that the municipal activists from every jurisdiction are recognized by public officials in other Quad-City jurisdictions.

One component of the ability to influence political behavior and achieve access to decision-makers is to be recognized. At this level, it is clear, the municipal activists in the Quad-City area are widely known beyond their own jurisdiction lines.

TABLE 40

MEAN NUMBER OF OFFICIALS FROM OTHER QUAD-CITY JURISDICTIONS
WHO IDENTIFY MUNICIPAL ACTIVISTS NOMINATED
FROM EACH JURISDICTION

Jurisdiction	Mean Number of Officials From Other Jurisdictions Identifying Municipal Activists From Each Jurisdiction
Davenport	42.8
Rock Island	38.8
Moline	81.8
East Moline	93.0
Bettendorf	29.3
Silvis	25.7
Milan	33.7
Carbon Cliff	31.3
Hampton	38.7
Riverdale	58.3

The two level of responses indicates a fuller measure of *political access.* This measure involves not only identification but also either having talked municipal affairs with the municipal activist, or having direct contact with him through clubs, social organizations, etc. Here the public officials from other jurisdictions also indicate that municipal activists were involved beyond their own jurisdiction lines. The municipal activist averages two-level activity or above with 20.2 officials from other jurisdictions. The range of responses at the two or better level is from 57 public officials indicating such contact down to only three. But not a *single one* of the municipal activists was isolated from some access at the two level to public officials in other Quad-City jurisdictions. In this measured sense, it is clear that many of the municipal activists are politically active to the extent of having access to public officials in jurisdictions other than their own.

The nominated municipal activists from large cities are reported to have access at the two level with a mean of 22.6 officials from other jurisdictions, compared to a mean of 16.9 other officials for the small jurisdiction municipal activists.

Table 41 presents the average number of public officials from other jurisdictions who report two level political access by the municipal activists from each jurisdiction. The East Moline nominated municipal activists have the most interjurisdictional political access, while the Hampton nominees are assessed the lowest on this score. No jurisdiction's nominees come close to being without interjurisdictional political access.

The public officials who report contact with municipal activists at the three level or above are reporting not only *political access*, but a degree of *political involvement* as well.

TABLE 41

MEAN NUMBER OF OFFICIALS FROM OTHER QUAD-CITY JURISDICTIONS
WHO INDICATE SCORES OF TWO OR MORE ("POLITICAL ACCESS")
FOR MUNICIPAL ACTIVISTS NOMINATED
FROM EACH JURISDICTION

Jurisdiction	Mean Number of Officials From Other Jurisdictions Indicating Scores of Two or More
Davenport	16.0
Rock Island	17.0
Moline	31.3
East Moline	35.8
Bettendorf	13.3
Silvis	12.7
Milan	14.0
Carbon Cliff	13.7
Hampton	12.0
Riverdale	32.0

Quad-City officials from jurisdictions other than those from which the municipal activists were nominated indicate that the 35 nominees have political involvement at the three level, with an average of 8.7 public officers each from other jurisdictions. These municipal activists are politically involved, by this operational measure, beyond the bounds of their own jurisdiction. The range of three level political involvement is from action with 27 other jurisdiction officials, for a Riverdale municipal activist, down to one municipal activist from Davenport who was not reported as having any three level influence with the respondents from other jurisdictions. Once again the nominated municipal activists from large cities are somewhat more often indicated to be politically involved with the other jurisdictions' officials than the small jurisdiction ones (a mean of 9.6 other public officials indicate three level involvements with large city municipal activists, compared to a mean of 7.5 for the small jurisdiction municipal activists).

The combined municipal activists from each of the ten jurisdictions evidence extensive political involvement with municipal officials in other jurisdictions. Table 42 presents the average number of public officials from other jurisdictions who report three level political involvement with the nominees from each separate city. Riverdale municipal activists are the most extensively involved at this level, and Carbon Cliff municipal activists the least extensively involved.

Any cumulative scores of four or more on this sequence of questions is defined as representing a level of major political involvement. The 35 municipal activists are reported to be involved to a major extent with public officials in other jurisdictions than their own, with an average of 4.2 such officials per municipal activist. The maximum number of officials reporting four or five level contact with any municipal activist is 15 for a person nominated from Riverdale. Only two municipal activists, both from Davenport, are reported to have no major political involvement relations with officials from other jurisdictions.

TABLE 42

MEAN NUMBER OF PUBLIC OFFICIALS FROM OTHER QUAD-CITY
JURISDICTIONS WHO INDICATE SCORES OF THREE OR MORE
("POLITICAL INVOLVEMENT") FOR MUNICIPAL ACTIVISTS
NOMINATED FROM EACH JURISDICTION

Jurisdiction	Mean Number of Officials From Other Jurisdictions Indicating Scores of Three or More
Davenport	6.3
Rock Island	8.3
Moline	11.8
East Moline	14.5
Bettendorf	7.3
Silvis	7.0
Milan	5.3
Carbon Cliff	3.0
Hampton	4.0
Riverdale	18.0

The large city municipal activists average only slightly more extensive extrajurisdictional major political involvement than the small jurisdiction municipal activists (a mean of 4.4 reports for large city municipal activists; a mean of 3.9 reports for small jurisdiction municipal activists).

Even at this four or five level, no jurisdiction's nominees are shut off from major political involvement beyond their own borders. Table 43 presents the average number of respondents indicating a major political involvement with the nominees from each of the jurisdictions.

The amount of four and five level "major political involvement" reports are found to be substantial. Their existence at all seemed quite unclear, and even unlikely as this research was initially formulated. These nominated municipal activists, with only two exceptions, are found to have been engaged in a high level of political action in jurisdictions other than their own.

TABLE 43

MEAN NUMBER OF PUBLIC OFFICIALS FROM OTHER QUAD-CITY
JURISDICTIONS WHO INDICATE SCORES OF FOUR OR FIVE
("MAJOR POLITICAL INVOLVEMENT") FOR MUNICIPAL
ACTIVISTS FROM EACH JURISDICTION

Jurisdiction	Mean Number of Officials From Other Jurisdictions Indicating Scores of Four or Five
Davenport	2.8
Rock Island	5.0
Moline	5.0
East Moline	6.3
Bettendorf	3.0
Silvis	3.3
Milan	1.7
Carbon Cliff	1.3
Hampton	2.3
Riverdale	10.7

On the basis of this analysis of the political role of 35 nominated municipal activists, it is possible to make some assertions relating to the general questions of this book. Do influential people play any mediating or otherwise integrating role in maintaining the plural political community? The answer is a clear yes. The nominated municipal activists are certainly classifiable as influential people within their own jurisdiction. They turn out to be widely known by public officials in other jurisdictions within the metropolitan area. Not only are they widely known, which is perhaps preliminary to the possibility of being influential, but they are found to have extensive political access to the public officials in other jurisdictions.

The responses of the public officials indicate that the nominated municipal activists also actually tend to be involved and frequently to evidence major involvement, as these are operationally defined, with almost no exceptions. They do deal with the public officials in other jurisdictions.

This evidence abundantly demonstrates that many of the active and influential citizens of one jurisdiction within the Quad-Cities are also active and influential in other jurisdictions. This is enough to say that they have *the ability* to overtly coordinate political action within separate jurisdictions. But even more than this, with nothing but anecdotal evidence of efforts at direct overt coordination, the fact that the mix of influences upon the official decision-makers in the separate cities are overlapping is proof of the fact that the separate jurisdictions do not act autonomously. These municipal activists, it seems clear, are not making *inconsistent* or *conflicting* demands upon the separate jurisdictions and their officials. Even without officials from separate cities coming into direct contact with one another, many potential sources of conflict are avoided, and many programs are able to operate in an integrated fashion. This can be accounted for, to an important degree, because the political structure of the separate jurisdictions includes actors who are also enmeshed in the political structure of the other jurisdictions.

In addition to wanting to know the *amount* of interjurisdictional influence activity of the municipal activists, it is also important to assess the *pattern* of this activity. Are the municipal activists characteristically active in only a single other Quad-City jurisdiction, or do they operate throughout the metropolitan area? What barrier does the Mississippi River pose? All of the questions which occurred with regard to the direct transaction measures are important here as well.

But there is one important difficulty. The first step selection process, and particularly the cut-off point at four or three municipal activists per jurisdiction, makes it somewhat hazardous to analyze the *patterns* of interjurisdictional influential activity. If more municipal activists had been selected, perhaps other patterns would occur. This seems a serious enough limitation so that no individual jurisdiction comparisons will be attempted (Davenport–Rock Island, etc.). But the sample seems large enough so that it is useful to compare the influence activity of municipal activists by the different groups of jurisdictions (big city–big city and small jurisdiction–small jurisdiction, interstate–intrastate, etc.).

The earlier analysis in this chapter involved an assessment of influence activity of the 35 nominees vis-à-vis individual public officials from the other jurisdictions. In order to undertake an analysis of the *patterns* of activity, it was decided that a municipal activist would be coded as being politically active in a jurisdiction, if at least three of the officials from that jurisdiction indicated second level ("political access") or higher contact with the municipal activist. This seemed a reasonable cut-off point, and in being reported at this level by at least three municipal officials of a jurisdiction would seem to indicate a fair amount of political activity there.

By this measure the 35 municipal activists are politically active in jurisdictions other than from which they were nominated some 96 times. Thus they average being politically active in 2.7 other jurisdictions. Only three municipal activists do not prove to be politically active by this measure, with any other jurisdiction than their own. One municipal activist, from East Moline, was found to be politically active in eight of the nine other jurisdictions. The municipal activists, then, are characteristically politically active in almost three other jurisdictions besides their own.

When this measure of political activity is used to see in what size other jurisdictions the municipal activists are involved, the results are quite interesting. Table 44 presents the average number of municipal activists from big cities and small jurisdictions who are politically active in the other large and smaller sized jurisdictions. The municipal activists nominated from the five large cities average being politically active in almost two and one-half other large jurisdictions, but they are politically active in the small jurisdictions far less frequently. The small jurisdictions' nominees are not often politically active in other small jurisdictions. On the other hand, they are

TABLE 44

DISTRIBUTION OF MEAN "POLITICAL ACTIVITY" OF MUNICIPAL
ACTIVISTS IN OTHER QUAD-CITY JURISDICTIONS
BY SIZE OF JURISDICTIONS

Direction of Relationship	Reported Political Activity	Number of Municipal Activists	Mean Political Activity of Municipal Activists
Big city Municipal Activists			
With other big cities	48	20	2.4
With small jurisdictions	10	20	.5
Small jurisdiction Municipal Activists			
With big cities	25	15	1.7
With other small jurisdictions	8	15	.5

characteristically active in more than one large city. Thus it seems fair to say that the large cities are relatively open to outside influence from people in surrounding jurisdictions, large and small. But this is not true for the small jurisdictions. The nominated municipal activists from small jurisdictions are much more extensively involved in political activity with large cities than they are with the other small jurisdictions. While the small jurisdictions' nominees are quite active politically in the large cities of the area, the municipal activists from the large cities are not nearly as extensively active in the political life of the small jurisdictions. Thus the pattern of political involvement of the municipal activists is quite similar to the patterns of direct exchange between the different size jurisdictions, with the notable addition that the small jurisdictions seem to operate with far less outside political activity by municipal activists than do the large cities.

Contiguity is a very important factor in the distribution of political activity by municipal activists in other jurisdictions. Fifty-two out of the 74 possible patterns of political activity by municipal activists with another contiguous jurisdiction actually are found to occur. This amounts to 70.3 per cent of the possibilities. This contrasts with 44/241, or 18.3 per cent of all noncontiguous incidents of interjurisdictional political activity by the municipal activists. The municipal activists are almost four times as likely to be politically involved in a contiguous jurisdiction as they are a noncontiguous one. The incidence of interjurisdictional political activity by municipal activists among the satellite-sun combinations is not stronger than the other contiguous relations. Nineteen of the 28 possible occurrences are found, or 67.9 per cent. The nominees from these small jurisdictions are politically active in the large cities (the "suns") in eleven of the twelve cases, but the large city municipal activists are only politically active in the satellites for eight of the 16 possible combinations.

The municipal activists are often politically involved in jurisdictions in the opposite Quad-City-area state. Iowa nominees are involved in Illinois jurisdictions, and vice versa. Twenty-six cases occur in which a municipal activist is found to be politically active in a jurisdiction in the other state from which he was nominated. This is out of a total *possible* number of 149. So 17.4 per cent of the possible combinations of interstate political action occur. This compares to 70 out of a possible 166, or 42.2 per cent, of the possible cases of intrastate political activity by municipal activists which actually occur. Thus, while much political activity is found which jumps the Mississippi River border, it is about two and one-half times more likely that a municipal activist will be politically involved in another jurisdiction within the same state.

In almost all respects the patterns of interjurisdictional political activity by these nominated municipal activists fall into the same patterns of exchange among the jurisdictions as did the direct exchanges. Big city–small city exchanges are in the familiar pattern. Contiguity and the state border are, once again, important factors in explaining the patterns which occur.

The municipal activists of the separate cities have been found to be politically active in other jurisdictions within the Quad-City area. They exhibit varying degrees of political involvement with the officials in these other jurisdictions. But their political activity is substantial, by any account. These findings help to explain the continued existence of the plural political community. Not only are there substantial and overlapping direct exchanges among the Quad-City public officials, but the political life of the separate jurisdictions is far from autonomous. Many of the same individuals who are most active in one jurisdiction turn out to be very much involved in the political life of other Quad-City jurisdictions.

INTEREST GROUPS

Many of the major associational groups in the Quad-City area are organized on an area basis. To the extent that these groups are involved in making demands upon the separate jurisdictions and are otherwise involved in their political life, they will be serving an integrative function within the metropolitan community. This section discusses the patterns of political involvement of some of the major interest articulating groups which are organized on a multijurisdictional basis in the Quad-Cities.[8]

The procedure used in this survey was to compile a list of area-wide associational groups in the Quad-Cities which seemed likely to be politically involved. This list was compiled from telephone directories, newspaper stories, and personal interviews with informants, and does not include all the area-wide groups that exist. It may omit some which should have been included, upon the basis of their activity, and it probably includes some that should have been omitted.[9]

8. Even when interest articulating groups are not organized on a multijurisdictional basis they may serve to integrate activities if separately organized groups of the same persuasion exist in the different jurisdictions. They may be making consistent demands, perhaps based on a nationally applicable program, on the separate governments. The extent to which this occurs in the Quad-City area has not been studied.

9. There is remarkably little information available upon the activities of interest groups in urban areas. Most urban studies of influence activity have operated on the premise that influence was the product of personal resources rather than associational ones. Sayre and Kaufman develop a useful typology of interest groups involved in New York City,

Even with the acknowledged difficulty of compiling an adequate list, the author believes that the list includes the major organized interest groups of the Quad-Cities. They include most of the usual spectrum of interest groups found at the state and federal levels. (General business groups, special business groups, organized labor, civil rights, and church groups.) A number of these are, on the surface, probably of the type that Sayre and Kaufman identify as most active—"frequent intervention in a narrow range of decisions"—but many also may be involved in "frequent intervention in a broad variety of decisions." Sayre and Kaufman indicated that this type of group was rare in New York City. Although this list may not be entirely adequate, if these particular groups play an interjurisdictional role in the political life of the Quad-Cities, that will be sufficient evidence that interest groups in general can and do perform an integrative function, whatever the omission.

The organized interest articulating groups which comprised the list are as follows:

1. Iowa-Illinois Industrial Development Group
2. Associated Industries of the Quad-Cities
3. Quad-City Association of Chamber of Commerce Presidents
4. Quad-City Technical Advisory Group
5. Dairy Council of the Quad-Cities, Inc.
6. Iowa-Illinois Marketers Association
7. Milk Foundation of the Quad-Cities
8. Quad-City Builders Association
9. Quad-City Electrical Contractors Association
10. Quint-Cities Sheet Metal Contractors Association
11. Quad-Cities Federation of Labor
12. Tri-Cities Building Trade Council
13. Council of Churches of Rock Island and Scott Counties
14. Mississippi Valley Association of Evangelicals
15. Tri-Cities NAACP
16. Quad-City Council on Human Rights

These organized groups were listed upon a card which was handed to all

but there is very little else upon which to base a listing of urban interest groups. See Wallace S. Sayre and Herbert Kaufman, *Governing New York City: Politics in the Metropolis* (New York: Russell Sage Foundation, 1960), pp. 760–786. William L. C. Wheaton does some valuable theorizing on the role of interest groups and other influence constellations in metropolitan areas, but his assumptions are clearly not tenable in the Quad-City area. See his "Integration at the Urban Level: Political Influence and the Decision Process," in Philip E. Jacob and James V. Toscano, eds., *The Integration of Political Communities* (Philadelphia and New York: J. B. Lippincott, 1964), pp. 120–142.

respondents to the interview schedule. The 227 public officials were asked two questions:

1. In connection with your work as a municipal official, have representatives of any of these associations ever called upon you with requests for information, advice, assistance, or other help with some issue or problem which any of these associations were concerned about?
2. In connection with your work as a municipal official, have you ever called upon representatives of any of these associations with requests for information, advice, assistance, or other help with some issue or problem you have been concerned with?

The answers to these questions are the data for this analysis.

These associations have been extensively involved with the Quad-City public officials. They average being reported as having dealings with 33.4 different public officials in the Quad-Cities. The range is from a total of one respondent indicating contact up to 66. The group listed as having only one contact is the only group which apparently has not been involved in any substantive contact with municipal officials. It is also the only case in which public officials from more than one jurisdiction do not indicate some contact with association representatives.

A prior decision was made, consistent with the similar decision regarding municipal activists, that if an organized interest group's representatives were listed as having had contact for their benefit or the jurisdiction's with at least three of the public officials from that jurisdiction, it would be classified as having been politically active there. Table 45 presents the results of this classification. By this measure all but two of these groups have been politically active in more than one jurisdiction within the Quad-City area. They average being politically active in 4.1 jurisdictions.

Political activity is heavily concentrated upon the large jurisdictions. Of 65 instances of such activity by these groups, 58 are in the large cities. The seven which are not are split between Silvis and Milan.

These organized interest groups are very much involved in the Quad-City political life, and characteristically so in many of the large cities. The political structure of the separate jurisdictions not only involves individuals (municipal activists) who are active in other jurisdictions, but organized interest groups as well. Interest group integrative activity is confined almost entirely to the large cities. The state border seems an unimportant factor here, for each interest group that has been politically active (14 of the original list of 16) has been active in jurisdictions on both sides of the Mississippi River. It is clear that the separate Quad-City jurisdictions do not have autonomous political lives. The activity of organized interest groups helps account for the maintenance of the Quad-City political community.

TABLE 45

"POLITICAL ACTIVITY" (REPORTED CONTACT WITH AT LEAST THREE OFFICIALS) OF QUAD-CITY AREA INTEREST ARTICULATING GROUPS FOR EACH JURISDICTION

Interest Group	JURISDICTION									
	Davenport	Rock Island	Moline	East Moline	Bettendorf	Silvis	Milan	Carbon Cliff	Hampton	Riverdale
Iowa-Illinois Industrial Development Group	X	X	X	X	X		X			
Associated Industries of the Quad-Cities	X	X								
Quad-City Association of Chamber of Commerce Presidents	X	X	X	X						
Quad-City Technical Advisory Group	X	X	X							
Dairy Council of the Quad-Cities, Inc.	X	X	X	X						
Iowa-Illinois Marketers Assoc.										
Milk Foundation of the Quad-Cities	X	X	X							
Quad-City Builders Association	X	X	X	X	X	X				
Quad-City Electrical Contractors Association	X	X	X	X	X	X				
Quint-Cities Sheet Metal Contractors Association	X	X	X	X	X	X	X			
Quad-Cities Federation of Labor	X	X	X	X	X	X				
Tri-Cities Building Trade Council	X	X	X	X	X		X			
Council of Churches of Rock Island and Scott Counties	X	X	X	X	X					
Mississippi Valley Association of Evangelicals										
Tri-Cities NAACP	X	X	X	X						
Quad-City Council on Human Rights	X	X	X	X						

While the role of interest groups is relatively unexplored in studies of urban political communities, the same cannot be said for the role of major corporations in American communities. Their role has been a theme of much controversial community power structure research.[10] But whatever the methodological approach, little evidence is available about what kind of an integrative role the corporations and industries of a metropolitan area might play in their community. The rather consistent findings that there is less local political activity by absentee-owned firms, or by modern corporations generally, when contrasted to older locally and family-owned manufacturers, would suggest a rather small political role generally in integrative affairs. Most of the major industries in the Quad-City area fit in the category of being nonlocally owned, with corporate rather than family management.[11] Thus they might be expected to be relatively uninvolved in integrative activities within the Quad-City political community. However, in the effort to be as comprehensive as possible, it was decided to explore this activity, small though it might be.

A list was compiled of the major manufacturing concerns in the Quad-City area. The list included all firms employing 1,000 or more employees, plus the Caterpillar Tractor Company. This firm has one installation in Riverdale and another being built outside Davenport which would boost employment much over the 1,000 level. In addition the Iowa-Illinois Gas and Electric Company, serving the whole area and one of the major taxpayers, plus the three daily newspaper organizations were included in the list. This list of fifteen included: Aluminum Company of America; AMETEK, Inc.; Bendix Corporation; J. I. Case and Company; Caterpillar Tractor Company; John Deere and Company; International Harvester; Iowa-Illinois Gas and Electric Company; Oscar Mayer and Company; Rock

10. See, for example, Delbert C. Miller, "Industry and Community Power Structure," *American Sociological Review* 23 (February 1958), 9–15; Roland J. Pellegrin and Charles H. Coates, "Absentee-Owned Corporations and Community Power Structure," *American Journal of Sociology* 61 (March 1956), 413–419; Robert O. Schultze, "The Bifurcation of Power in a Satellite City," in Morris Janowitz, ed., *Community Political Systems* (New York: Free Press of Glencoe, 1961). Nelson W. Polsby works these studies over rather thoroughly in *Community Power and Political Theory* (New Haven: Yale University Press, 1963).

11. Deere and Co. is still partially managed and controlled by the family of John Deere, and it displays a good deal of community concern. The farm equipment industry generally has tended to consider the Quad-City area as something of a home base for the prairie and plains states. For an excellent discussion of the role of Deere and Co. in the area, see Gene Bylinsky, "Farm Technology Plows Ahead at Deere," *Fortune*, December 1966, pp. 147–151, 278–280.

Island Arsenal; Rock Island or Union Pacific Railroad; Servus Rubber Company; Davenport Newspapers, Inc. (other than newsmen); Moline Daily Dispatch (other than newsmen); Rock Island Argus (other than newsmen). The list was presented to all the public officials, and they were asked essentially the same two questions as were asked about dealings with organized interest groups:

> Here is a list of Quad-City area corporations. In connection with your work as a municipal official, have representatives of any of these firms ever called upon you with requests for information, advice, assistance, or other help with some issue or problem they were concerned about?

> In connection with your work as a municipal official, have you ever called upon representatives of any of these firms with requests for information, advice, assistance, or other help with any issue or problem you have been concerned with?

The public officials indicated that representatives of these firms have been quite active in the affairs of the Quad-City jurisdictions. The 15 manufacturing firms average dealings with 48.3 Quad-City officials. Thus the corporations have a considerably greater range of dealings with Quad-City officials than the organized interest groups (who average dealings with 33.4 public officials). Each of the firms on the list has been involved in contact with public officials in more than one Quad-City jurisdiction. In fact, there is some reported contact with each of the 15 firms in Davenport, Rock Island, Moline, and Bettendorf.

It was decided to apply the same measure of contact used in the study of municipal activists and interest groups. Contact with at least three officials from a jurisdiction is used as the measure of active participation in that jurisdiction. Once again dealings with three officials seemed like a reasonable prior choice as an indicator of political activity of some importance within a jurisdiction. Table 46 presents the extent of participation activity and this level for the 15 corporations and industrial firms with the separate jurisdictions.

These corporations and industrial firms are very active, by this measure, with Quad-City jurisdictions. They rate as being politically involved with an average of 4.7 Quad-City jurisdictions. This represents a broader involvement for the corporations and industrial firms than the organized interest groups which average dealings with 4.1 jurisdictions.

Every one of the listed firms are politically active in some Quad-City jurisdiction, and only Servus Rubber is not reported as being involved in more than one jurisdiction. One firm is reported as being active in all ten

TABLE 46

"POLITICAL ACTIVITY" (REPORTED CONTACT WITH AT LEAST THREE OFFICIALS) OF QUAD-CITY AREA CORPORATIONS AND MANUFACTURING FIRMS FOR EACH JURISDICTION

Corporations and Manufacturing Firms	JURISDICTION									
	Davenport	Rock Island	Moline	East Moline	Bettendorf	Silvis	Milan	Carbon Cliff	Hampton	Riverdale
Aluminum Co. of America	X									X*
AMETEK, Inc.		X	X	X*	X					
Bendix Corporation	X	X			X					
J. I. Case and Company	X	X*			X*					
Caterpillar Tractor Company	X	X			X					X*
John Deere and Company	X	X*	X*	X*	X	X	X			
International Harvester	X	X*	X	X*	X	X				
Iowa-Illinois Gas and Electric Company	X	X	X	X	X	X	X	X	X	X
Oscar Mayer and Company	X*	X*	X							
Rock Island Arsenal	X	X	X	X	X	X	X	X		
Rock Island or Union Pacific Railroad	X	X	X	X	X	X	X	X		
Servus Rubber Company		X*								
Davenport Newspapers, Inc. (other than newsmen)	X*	X	X	X	X					
Moline Daily Dispatch (other than newsmen)	X	X	X*	X						
Rock Island Argus (other than newsmen)	X	X*	X		X					

* Site of major facility

jurisdictions, but that is something of a special case, for the Iowa-Illinois Gas and Electric Company provides utility service to all ten jurisdictions. But in addition the firm is a major taxpayer (representatives of the firm say it is the major property taxpayer in the Quad-City area), is deeply involved in industrial development work, and is otherwise involved in the area's political life. It was not possible to separate out these different activities.

The other organizations with the widest scope of political activity are the Rock Island Arsenal, Rock Island Railroad (and Union Pacific, then lobbying locally for merger with the Rock Island Line), both with eight jurisdictions, and Deere and Company, with seven jurisdictions. Fifty-five of the 70 incidences of political activity by corporations and industrial firms are with large cities (73.3 per cent of the *possible* incidents of political activity with large cities). Fifteen of the incidents of political activity are with small jurisdictions (20.0 per cent of the *possible* incidents). Thus the corporations are very active in other large jurisdictions, but much less politically active in the small jurisdictions in the Quad-Cities.

While many of these firms have facilities in more than one Quad-City jurisdiction, the political involvement is not limited to those jurisdictions in which the firms are located. Alcoa is not even reported as being politically active in the jurisdiction in which it is located, although it is active elsewhere. This probably can be explained by the character of the Riverdale government, with its exceedingly low tax and minimal municipal services. (Alcoa is deeply involved in the politics of the independent school district in which it is located.) Only four of the 15 firms confine their political activity to jurisdictions in a single state.

The three newspapers are all involved in political activity in other jurisdictions, but only with other large cities. Neither the Moline or Rock Island papers are reported as being politically active in Davenport, but the Davenport based newspaper (which publishes an Illinois edition) is active in all of the large cities of the area.

It seems clear that the corporations and industrial firms of the area are politically active in the separate jurisdictions to the extent that they are a factor in the maintenance of this political community. They are actually substantially more active in this than are the area-wide interest groups. They, like the interest groups, are mostly active in the five large cities. By their demands and other involvement in the political and governmental affairs of the separate cities, they insure that the jurisdictions do not act out of concert on many items. Together with the municipal activists and interest groups they create a single metropolitan political system, in which the jurisdictional subsystems are relatively well-meshed. Thus the activities of the separate jurisdictions are integrated by more than the direct exchanges between the jurisdictions and the public officials in the Quad-

Cities. They are also integrated by the indirect effect of having political structures in which the individuals, interest groups, and major corporations and industrial firms who are involved in the jurisdiction's political life are also involved in the other municipalities. This indirect integration is considerably more extensive among the large cities than it is among the small jurisdictions. But it is important throughout the Quad-City area.[12]

NEWSMEN AS PERSONAL INTERMEDIARIES BETWEEN JURISDICTIONS

The newsmen who cover municipal governmental and political affairs for the newspapers and the radio and television stations are frequently found around the different city halls in the Quad-Cities. Many of the same newsmen upon occasion cover events occurring in the different area jurisdictions, and appear to play some personal intermediary role between the different jurisdictions.

This integrative role seems at least possible because newsmen who cover political and govermental affairs are usually among the best informed "outsiders" with regard to those governments' activities. They are often, in fact, key confidants of public officials. If the Quad-City area newsmen are highly informed about activities of the separate jurisdictions, and have developed close ties to public officials in the separate cities, they can serve in an advisory or information transmitting capacity between the jurisdictions and public officials whom they cover.

With other jurisdictions so handy for comparison of programs and activities, it is likely that newsmen as legitimate and regular interrogators of public figures in the different jurisdictions would serve to keep officials informed of activity going on elsewhere. An example of the potential role of newsmen as interjurisdictional actors occurred in 1966 when Davenport police officers caught some parking meter thieves in a stakeout. Newsmen

12. For both the interest groups and the corporations and industrial firms, the decision to list an organization as politically active in a jurisdiction if it has been involved with at least three officials may, in retrospect, seem too low a threshold. But it would not have been a proper research method to change this list once the data had been looked at. If the measure of *political activity* had been set at five instead of three, interest groups would have been listed as active in 53 jurisdictions (instead of 65) and corporations would have been listed as active in 50 jurisdictions, rather than 70. But all of the generalizations from this categorization would stand unchanged.

These data are a reasonably good rough indicator of involvement of interest groups and corporations, although *frequency* of political activity rather than *scope* is arguably a better measure. These data seem to provide sufficient indicators to test the major questions in this section.

immediately, and apparently routinely, inquired at the other major jurisdictions whether they too had been losing money in the meters. In doing this they served to inform the other jurisdictions of the event in Davenport. If this type of occurrence is regular, it may be an important element in the metropolitan political community. Activities may sometimes be integrated in this manner without the need of direct exchange between public officials from the separate units.

In order to explore the potential role of newsmen as intermediaries between the Quad-City jurisdictions, all of the public officials who were interviewed were asked two questions:

Can you recall, do you ever use any of the newsmen who interview you about city affairs as a source for getting personal or confidential information about activities in any of the other Quad-City area local governments?

Can you recall, do newsmen ever contact you for information concerning news items which initially arise in other Quad-City area governments, in order to compare their information with what the situation is in your city?

Thirty-four Quad-City officials indicated that they did use newsmen as a source of personal or confidential information about activities in other jurisdictions. While this is only a small per cent of all the officials (15.0 per cent), it seems likely that newsmen are also informants in other instances in which the public officials are not overtly querying the newsmen. The 34 officials reporting instances of this type of activity are a fairly high per cent of the officials who are in regular contact with newsmen. Many of the interviewed public officials have only rare occasions to meet the newsmen at all.

Twenty-nine officials from large cities report this use of the newsmen, but only five of the officials from small jurisdictions do so. This is surely a reflection of the fact that the reporters from the major news media rarely cover activities in the small jurisdictions. The newspapers tend to rely upon local "stringers" who report the news from these individual municipalities in the manner in which "neighborhood news" columns are printed in many papers.

Eighty-six of the public officials report that newsmen contact them about news items arising in other jurisdictions for comparison purposes. Thus, a substantial number of occurrences in other jurisdictions apparently are brought to the attention of public officials by the newsmen. The newsmen serve as personal information transmitters between jurisdictions simply as a latent consequence of their newsgathering activities.

The newsmen are reported as performing this activity with 71 of the large city officials, and 15 small jurisdiction officials. Once again this disparity is surely a consequence of the fact that regular newsmen are comparatively inactive in the small jurisdictions.

Newsmen are generally quite important actors in American politics. In the Quad-Cities they turn out to play an important, if minor, role in the integration of political activity. They are an element in the metropolitan political system. The newsmen act as personal information transmitters between officials in these different jurisdictions, and particularly between the larger cities. The newsmen's product, their stories, may also be an important source of information transmittal, but was not explored in the study.

Municipal Consultants and the Metropolitan System

In recent years consultant firms have supplied many services to local governments. While bonding consultants and planning and engineering consultant firms are probably most numerous, local governments contract for a wide array of outside advice and plans. A cursory inspection of the advertising in any state municipal league journal is enough evidence that consultants come in many and various competences. They are frequently used in the Quad-City area.

It seemed possible that these municipal entrepreneurs might have some part to play in the political integration of the Quad-City area. If the jurisdictions in the area have come to rely upon the same set of outside paid advisors, these consultants might be facilitating the maintenance of the political community because the consultants in their plans and proposals would have special knowledge of what the other local governments were about. Perhaps because of their desire to see their own plans and proposals succeed in all the jurisdictions in which they worked, they would actually serve a fairly direct coordinating role. At least they would probably see that avoidable conflicts in planning or needless duplication of effort were minimized. Because the consultants propose programs and projects which are in fact acted upon, they themselves are reasonably important decision-makers in the separate jurisdictions in which they work. If they work for more than one jurisdiction, some fairly consistent programs may result. Even the profit nexus could support integrative efforts. If a profit making corporation employed by one jurisdiction wanted to maintain or develop a business association with other local governments, it would be incumbent upon it to avoid plans and recommendations which would conflict with plans of these other local jurisdictions.

This all seems plausible, but needs evidence which is not presently available. What is available from the Quad-City survey is the list of consultant firms used by the various Quad-City jurisdictions. If it turns out that a set of consultant firms does operate throughout the area, further research surely will be warranted. This phenomenon, if it exists, may also contribute to the maintenance of the political community.

All respondents were asked to list all the consulting firms they knew their jurisdiction had employed. This list was culled of duplicates for each jurisdiction and amounted to a total of 66 separate consulting firms. The large cities are apparently much more prone to use these firms than are the smaller jurisdictions. The five large cities indicate using 76 consultants, while the small jurisdiction respondents report only 15. Davenport respondents listed 23 different consulting firms for the most, while Hampton and Riverdale only indicate a single such association.

Eleven of the listed firms are reported as serving more than one Quad-City jurisdiction. While six of these are used only in two jurisdictions, two different planning and engineering firms were listed as consultants to six Quad-City jurisdictions. The remaining three were used in three jurisdictions.

The firms in operation in more than one Quad-City jurisdiction were mostly engineering and planning consultants (eight), with one bonding consultant and two public administration type firms. Thus, if these municipal consultants are playing a coordinating role, it is probably most important in capital improvements and planning—the areas in which there is the most extensive multiple use of consultants. The two planning and engineering firms which have been used by six of the jurisdictions may be particularly crucial in the metropolitan scene. For in addition to being used widely, they are also used for a greater number of separate projects per city than any of the other firms. They are both located within a close distance of the Quad-Cities so that they are a permanent element in the metropolitan political community. They, in particular, may be contributing to the political integration of the Quad-City political community.

CONCLUSION

In earlier chapters the direct exchanges between the political jurisdictions of the Quad-City area have been seen to be extensive and important in maintaining the plural political community. It now is clear that the integration of activity also occurs without direct exchanges between the jurisdictions and their public officials. The separate jurisdictions do not have autonomous political life. People who are active in an individual jurisdiction are found to be politically active elsewhere in the metropolitan area. Interest groups and corporations as interest articulating organizations are politically active throughout the metropolitan area. Through their involvement and activities in the separate jurisdictions, these individuals and groups help account for the maintenance of the political community. The newsmen have also been depicted as involved in activity with integrative consequences for the metropolitan area. Perhaps the activity of consulting firms used by the municipalities is also of some importance.

By all of these types of activity the programs of the separate jurisdictions become subject to outside metropolitan influence. This occurs even without direct contact between the public officials. These indirect exchanges are much more extensive among the large cities than they are among the small jurisdictions. They are a major factor in the large cities, but probably of only supplemental importance with the small jurisdictions. These separate jurisdictions operate in a complex and highly interrelated metropolitan political structure, in which there are regular and systematic direct and indirect exchanges among the municipalities which serve to maintain the political community.

7

Specialization, Competition, and Conflict

There are some other crucial elements of the Quad-City metropolitan political community. This chapter discusses the political integration of activities which may occur without overt coordination, either direct or indirect. It also considers the use of other jurisdictions' experience when making decisions for a municipality, and assesses the occurrence of competition among the ten municipalities. Finally, the chapter analyzes the occurrences and consequences of interjurisdictional conflict which may be found in the Quad-City area. These subjects concern how the metropolitan system and the individual jurisdictions maintain themselves and remain responsive, adjustable, and satisfactory to citizens in the face of jurisdictional diffusion, with formally independent governments in close proximity to each other.

Mutual Adjustment

As Charles Lindblom has argued, some integration of political activity may occur without any direct or indirect overt coordination.[1] It may occur simply by virtue of the fact that public officials know what the neighboring jurisdictions are doing, and take this into account in their own decision-making. This may result in reducing unnecessary overlapping of services and may lead to an avoidance of unnecessary conflict.

The power of a "mutual adjustment" process, without overt coordination, in partially explaining the continued existence of a metropolitan political community seems a very difficult measure to assess. Ultimately, it is probably not adequately surveyed with a questionnaire or interview schedule. For much "mutual adjustment" activity may occur below the threshold

1. Charles E. Lindblom, *The Intelligence of Democracy: Decision Making Through Mutual Adjustment* (New York: Free Press of Glencoe, 1965).

of conscious design. For example, a city council may never consider building a public auditorium, because the councilmen "know" one is already provided in the metropolitan community by a neighboring jurisdiction. Thus the "mutual adjustment" process may explain why no overlapping and duplicating public auditorium is built. But no councilman may even be aware of making this "decision." This type of unconscious "mutual adjustment" may occur for myriad items, large and small.

There is a conscious element to some mutual adjustment activity which may be tapped by an interview, however. The Quad-City officials were asked about this in a series of questions. The mayors and councilmen were asked: "As a decision-maker for your city, do you ever specifically try to specialize your city services or activities, so that they *complement* or *fit in with* the services or activities of other Quad-City area local governments, rather than just duplicate services already available in these other cities?" The department and agency heads were asked an analogous question: "Has your department (agency) ever specifically tried to specialize any of your departmental (agency) services or activities so that they *complement* or *fit in with* the services or activities of other Quad-City local governments, rather than just to duplicate services already available in these other cities?"[2]

Only 30 of the 227 respondents indicated an awareness of any conscious specialization of this nature (13.2 per cent). Most of these (27) were from the five large cities.

The specific items listed by the respondents answering this question affirmatively cover a wide range, although most were fairly large projects. The two most frequently mentioned projects were the metropolitan airport and the bridges. The metropolitan airport serves the Quad-City community, but is run by the Illinois cities. Davenport has a small municipal airport geared for serving private airplanes. One of the bridges was built by Rock Island, another by Davenport. The Davenport Art Gallery serves the whole metropolis, and was also mentioned. Park programs were listed. The smaller items consisted of such things as one city maintaining a store of equipment parts which was available to other cities' maintenance crews.

In many of these listed cases the specialization was far from pure instances of "mutual adjustment" integration. For some items, there seemed to have been rather explicit direct bargaining. For others, a hierarchical decision

2. The wording of these questions was difficult, so the following explanation was always given the respondents: "For example a city might decide not to put in a municipal swimming pool, because other cities in the area already had swimming pools which were available for use. Instead it might put in some other recreation facility which was not available elsewhere. Or it might decide not to hire a lie detector operator, because another city already had one who was available for use. Instead it would get some other type of specialist which other Quad-City area local governments did not have. Can you recall, have you specifically ever tried to specialize your services in this way?"

structure was evident. This was found for some of the specialized park services, where the metropolitan planning agency approved federally assisted open space programs of the separate cities. This also occurred with the metropolitan airport, where federal agencies made the final decision. So the existence of conscious "mutual adjustment" integration of activities seems quite low by this measure.

Related questions shed some more light on the existence of conscious "mutual adjustment" decision-making. The 227 respondents were asked whether they could recall any services or activities provided by their department or agency or their city, in which they serve residents of other Quad-City jurisdictions so that those municipalities did not need to provide that service, or at least as much of it. Seventy-three officials, or 32.2 per cent of the respondents answered affirmatively. A somewhat higher per cent of big city officials (35.4 per cent) indicated they were providing services to others than small city officials (24.6 per cent). Mayors and councilmen were much more sensitive to this than were department or agency heads. Fifty-four per cent of the mayors and councilmen indicated that their government was providing services used by citizens of other jurisdictions, lessening those other jurisdictions' load. Only 19.4 per cent of the department heads and agency heads thought they were so providing services to others.

The mayors and councilmen were asked the reverse question as well. A much smaller per cent of mayors and councilmen acknowledged that their own government was not providing some service, but that the citizens were using the services available through another jurisdiction. Nineteen of 83 mayors and councilmen indicated that their jurisdiction did not provide some service, but the residents made use of that service in another jurisdiction. Most incidents of this kind which were mentioned were park and recreation services, with a few mentions of the metropolitan airport. Surprisingly, the large city officials acknowledged this situation much more readily than their small jurisdiction counterparts (15 of 37 large city officials, compared to four of 31 small jurisdictional officials).

These two questions proved to be the most sensitive ones in the interview schedule, especially with mayors and councilmen. Many elected officials displayed emotion when listing the uses of their city services by residents of other jurisdictions, and were vehement in denying any such activity by their own citizens. We speculate that many public officials, particularly elected ones, believe it seriously improper for a jurisdiction to rely on gratis services of another jurisdiction. They think the jurisdictions ought to provide for all the needs of their own citizens. This belief probably inhibits any large amount of conscious "mutual adjustment," as a vehicle for achieving economies of scale.

Unconscious "mutual adjustment" may be an important element in the maintenance of the plural political community of the Quad-Cities. But conscious "mutual adjustment" activity is quite limited, as measured in the study. It does not seem to be a major element in maintaining the plural political system.

One important way in which public officials might make use of their neighboring jurisdictions would be for them to rely on the experiences of their neighbors when considering some similar action in their own jurisdictions. Neighboring jurisdictions might be able to provide a repository of experiences which would prove most useful to municipal officials. The experience of Rock Island with its urban renewal program might provide substantial cues to Davenport, Moline, East Moline, and Milan as they prepare to follow suit, to list a major example. Comparing notes on a piece of road equipment before purchase, or on the reliability of a contractor, would be other possible instances in which one jurisdiction relied on the earlier experiences of another jurisdiction.

The Quad-City elected officials were asked: "Do you yourself look for examples of projects or activities carried out in any of the other Quad-City area local governments when deciding what decision you will make for your own municipality?" Appointed officials were asked the analogous question. Seventy-four per cent of the 227 officials indicated that they did look for examples to other Quad-City jurisdictions. The difference in responses between large city officials (75.3 per cent) and small jurisdiction officials (71.0 per cent) was minor. These Quad-City municipal decision-makers clearly rely upon experiences of the other jurisdictions for many things. The officials were also asked if they could recall recent instances of looking for examples in each of the other jurisdictions. Table 47 indicates the direction in which these officials look for examples, as between different size jurisdictions and among jurisdictions of the same size. Large city officials

TABLE 47

DIRECTION OF REPORTED USE OF EXAMPLES FROM OTHER QUAD-CITY
JURISDICTIONS AMONG DIFFERENT SIZED JURISDICTIONS

Direction of Use of Examples	Reported Occurrences	Possible Occurrences	Per Cent Which Occur
Big city to other big city	206	628	32.8
Big city–small jurisdiction	23	785	2.9
Small jurisdiction–big city	93	345	27.0
Small jurisdiction to other small jurisdiction	29	276	10.5
Total	351	2034	17.3

almost always look to other large cities for examples. Small jurisdiction officials rely mostly upon the large cities too.

Contiguous jurisdictions are looked to far more extensively (35.5 per cent of the *possible* reports) than are noncontiguous jurisdictions (11.5 per cent). Recent cases of looking for examples in jurisdictions across the Mississippi River state line are less common (13.0 per cent of the *possible* reports) than instances of looking for examples in the respondents' own state (21.8 per cent).

Officials from other jurisdictions indicate they have used examples from Rock Island more often than from any of the other cities. Table 48 lists the number and per cent of Quad-City officials who have looked at examples in each of the other jurisdictions. Rock Island, the only city manager government, may be viewed as the most professional of the city administrations, which may account for the frequent reliance upon its experience. But Rock Island also seems to start new programs ahead of the other cities. This is also something of a reverse measure of innovation from outside the Quad-City political community. The three largest cities seem to be the innovative leaders. Apart from Davenport, the larger the jurisdiction, the more other officials look to it for examples.

TABLE 48

REPORTED RECENT USE OF EXAMPLES FROM EACH OF
THE OTHER QUAD-CITY JURISDICTIONS

Jurisdiction	Number Using Examples	Number of other Officials	Per Cent Using Examples
Davenport	66	192	34.4
Rock Island	89	191	46.6
Moline	80	189	42.3
East Moline	50	200	25.0
Bettendorf	24	205	11.8
Silvis	23	208	11.0
Milan	10	213	4.7
Carbon Cliff	10	212	4.7
Hampton	5	216	2.3
Riverdale	4	217	1.8

The Quad-City officials seem to tap their counterparts' experience as a regular occurrence. This is probably an important element in keeping the jurisdictions in balance and in improving the quality of the services in the separate cities and throughout the area.

Competition among political jurisdictions is usually discussed in terms of dysfunctional consequences. For example, money may be needlessly spent on suburban sewer systems because of local pride and unwillingness to depend upon a central city, when economies of scale could be achieved by having a single sewer system for the metropolitan area. But competition among jurisdictions may also serve to improve the quality of services of the citizens of the separate jurisdictions. This may occur if, for example, public officials of neighboring jurisdictions try to outdo each other in their work. The Quad-City officials were asked a series of questions about the extent to which they consciously made efforts to keep up with or ahead of their counterparts. The particular subjects of such competition which were explored in the interview were level of services, budget requests and tax levies, and salaries of municipal officials.

The elected officials were asked, "Do you particularly try to compete by keeping up with or ahead of any of these other Quad-City area local governments in the level of services you provide your citizens?" Appointed officials were asked the analogous question in relation to their department or agency.

A great many officials report they do consciously compete with neighboring jurisdictions in providing services. Seventy-two officials (31.9 per cent of the respondents) answered "yes" to this question. Competition on services is slightly more common among large city officials (35.0 per cent) than their small jurisdiction counterparts (24.6 per cent). Table 49 presents the

TABLE 49

DIRECTION OF REPORTED COMPETITION IN PROVIDING SERVICES AMONG QUAD-CITY JURISDICTIONS FOR DIFFERENT SIZED JURISDICTIONS

Direction of Relationship	Reported Competition	Possible Competition	Per Cent Which Occur
Big city to other big city	161	628	25.6
Big city–small jurisdiction	64	785	8.2
Small jurisdiction–big city	44	345	12.8
Small jurisdiction to other small jurisdiction	27	276	9.8
Total	296	2034	14.6

direction of the competition between big cities and small jurisdictions and among jurisdictions in each of these categories. Officials from the large jurisdictions compare themselves with other large jurisdictions much more extensively than they do with the five smaller municipalities. This seems reasonable, of course, for jurisdictions of comparable size are most likely to have similar programs. But the small jurisdiction officials indicate that they look to the large cities more often than they do to other jurisdictions of their own size. This is probably the result of the comparative isolation of the small jurisdictions from each other, as found in the transaction measures in earlier chapters.

The effect of the river border is not substantial in regard to competition for services. Quad-City officials list themselves in competition over services with 12.4 per cent of the possible interstate combinations, as compared to 16.2 per cent of the intrastate possibilities. Contiguity is a more important differentiation. The respondents list competition with contiguous jurisdictions in 23.2 per cent of the possible combinations, compared to 11.4 per cent of the noncontiguous possibilities.

Slightly fewer Quad-City officials indicate that they are in conscious budgetary and tax level competition with other Quad-City jurisdictions. Fifty-four officials (226 respondents), or 23.9 per cent of them, indicate that this is conscious concern of theirs. This is more pronounced among large city officials (27.4 per cent) than among small jurisdiction officials (16.0 per cent). With no exceptions all other patterns are in the same direction and in similar strength to the patterns found for competition over providing services (data not reported).

The last item of potential competition which was questioned is over salaries paid to municipal officials. Fifty-one of the 79 elected officials (64.6 per cent) acknowledged that it was a conscious concern of theirs to keep salaries competitive with other Quad-City jurisdictions. An even higher per cent (68.4 per cent) of the elected officials said that the city officials and employees cited the salaries paid in other Quad-City jurisdictions when requesting salary increases. This salary competition is most consciously felt in the five larger cities, where 40 of the 49 officials list it. Eleven of the 30 elected officials in the small jurisdictions also list competition on salaries. Therefore, it is an important element throughout the Quad-City area. All patterns of earlier items of competition occur with competition over salary levels. Large city officials look to other large cities, and small jurisdiction officials look to the large cities also. The small jurisdictions are rarely looked to by either large or small jurisdiction officials (data not reported).

The Quad-City public officials frequently view themselves as being in competition of some sort with the other jurisdictions. This competition to maintain or improve their municipality's position vis-à-vis the other jurisdictions is most common for salaries, but it is also a concern of many officials for levels of service, budget askings and tax levies. All of these items of competition probably cause the jurisdictions to remain in some sort of balance as far as the levels of service they provide. Probably, no jurisdiction can get too far out of line with its neighbors. It is even reasonable to suppose that this feedback from the other jurisdictions would tend to improve the quality of public services in the separate jurisdictions. Public officials have unmistakable models to pattern programs after and compare with their own. Citizens can look to the other jurisdictions too. Although the extent to which residents compare services and make demands upon the jurisdictions upon the basis of such comparisons was unmeasured in this survey, the researcher's journal is full of anecdotes in which this occurred in his presence during the research project. For example, a radio "phone forum" would air complaints over municipal services in which a caller would be irate over the slowness of snow removal in his city, compared to another.

Thus, the municipalities and their officials are frequently in conscious competition with other jurisdictions. Much of this competition may actually improve public services in the metropolitan area. It also helps to maintain equilibrium among the separate jurisdictions and their program.

CONFLICT

The many case studies of conflict and conflict resolution among jurisdictions within metropolitan areas have conveyed a general impression that the different governments in metropolitan areas are characteristically sensitive, especially to any threats or slights, and usually engaged in rancorous encounters with neighboring jurisdictions. In this survey, it was decided to explore for the existence of interjurisdictional conflicts and their consequences in the Quad-City area. The discussion of consequences is necessarily foreshortened, for not enough actual conflicts were found to carry this analysis very far.

All public officials were asked if their jurisdiction had been engaged in any disputes or conflicts with any of the other Quad-City jurisdictions within the last year. By consensus of the respondents from the separate jurisdictions, three separate conflicts had occurred. Rock Island and Milan were involved in a complicated conflict involving, among other things, the fact that Rock Island had "jumped" the Rock River in annexation, cutting off some expansion possibilities for Milan. The immediate issue concerned Rock Island needing to run sewer lines across Milan property to serve its expanded area. The second issue or conflict was between Moline and East Moline, and it also involved competitive annexation, and the provision of services to newly annexed areas. Both of these conflicts were extensively covered in the press, and were seemingly quite bitter. In both cases there was complicated legal maneuvering, statements and counterstatements to the press, and even arrests. In both cases, police from one of the disputant governments actually arrested and jailed agents of their antagonist. To all outward appearances, these were major disruptive events, which seemed likely to unleash continuing and widespread serious consequences for relations between the parties. The third conflict was between Silvis and adjoining Carbon Cliff. Silvis maintained its sewage disposal plant within the village limits of Carbon Cliff, by virtue of a contractual agreement with an earlier village council. Carbon Cliff residents complained of terrible odors. Silvis denied that the sewage plant emitted odors (or very terrible odors anyway). Carbon Cliff took legal action enjoining operation of the plant, but later lifted the injunction on Silvis' agreement to improve conditions. But Carbon Cliff officials claimed that the situation did not improve. This dispute also involved the arrest of a Silvis official at the instigation of Carbon Cliff. These were the only conflicts between Quad-City jurisdictions upon which there was any mutual agreement as to their existence.

Three Davenport officials did list a conflict with Bettendorf over connecting Davenport and Bettendorf interceptor lines. No Bettendorf officials mentioned this, and probing indicated that the "conflict" was simply a negotiation stumbling block, with Bettendorf not moving as fast as the three Davenport officials would like. (The Davenport officials who actually conducted discussions with Bettendorf and who were administratively concerned with sewer interceptors did not interpret this situation as a conflict.) In addition, one Moline official listed another conflict with East Moline over the interpretation of a code provision on an ordinance both cities used. This was a minor and personal "conflict" involving one man's perception of the views of a counterpart.

The conflicts listed above were all those reported among the Quad-City public officials for the prior year. Nor were there any indications that this number was other than normal.

Interjurisdictional conflicts were not found to be extensive in the Quad-City area. But it is also vitally important to understand what consequences these conflicts have for relations between jurisdictions. What legacy do such conflicts leave?

All officials in the jurisdictions involved in conflict were asked whether they thought the resolution of that dispute would be satisfactory to their own government. (During the interview period, the Moline–East Moline conflict was effectively resolved, but the Rock Island–Milan and Silvis–Carbon Cliff situations were still unresolved.) Every single Moline and East Moline official who listed a conflict as existing between them (a total of 58 respondents) thought the solution of the conflict was satisfactory to his government. Not a single one felt his side had lost. In the ongoing

Milan–Rock Island dispute, fifteen Rock Island officials thought the solution would be satisfactory, while five did not. Eight did not know. Six Milan officials thought the solution would be satisfactory, while two did not. Six did not know. In spite of the recriminations in the press, and the arrests, fully three-quarters of the affected officials believed the problem would be satisfactorily solved. The Silvis–Carbon Cliff dispute received similar assessments from those public officials. Twelve of the 13 Silvis officials were satisfied, while one was not. Carbon Cliff officials were split much more. Six indicated a satisfactory solution was likely, two did not think so, and six did not know.

In spite of the public bitterness of all three of these disputes, the one which was resolved left no measurable aftertaste in attitudes. A large majority of the officials in the other two disputes also remain confident about the outcome. Little tendency has been uncovered to nurse grievances toward other jurisdictions, even during periods of public controversy.

The officials from disputing jurisdictions were also asked whether the disagreement affected their own relations with the other governments. The overwhelming majority of these officials indicated that the conflict did not affect their own relations with the other government. Fifteen of 135 officials indicated that the conflict affected their relations. One official each in Moline, Silvis, and Carbon Cliff indicated that the conflict affected them, as did two East Moline officials. Thus, the Rock Island–Milan dispute had most of the spillover consequences. Six Rock Island officials and four Milan officials said their relations were affected. By the measures which were applied in this study, the few interjurisdictional disputes which actually occurred had very little spillover consequences, even though any reading of the newspaper accounts of the events indicate they were very bitter disputes.

All three of the conflicts which have been found are between single jurisdictions. But many of the individual cases of interjurisdictional disputes reported in the literature deal with multiple jurisdiction conflicts. The metropolitan politics theory of countervailing forces of Winston Crouch and Beatrice Dinerman is based upon a persistent alliance of the small jurisdictions against the large jurisdictions.

The Quad-City respondents were asked two questions:

Insofar as you can recall, has your city ever joined forces with or worked jointly with any of the other Quad-City area local governments upon some issue or question, in which you were actually opposed to one of the other Quad-City area local governments?

Insofar as you recall, have any other Quad-City area local governments ever joined forces or worked jointly with other Quad-City area local governments upon some issue or question, in which they were actually opposed to the position of your city government?

The overwhelming number of officials could not think of any instances in which conflict occurred involving multiple jurisdictions or alliances. A few old-timers recalled that many years ago when the metropolitan airport was located in the Quad-City area, and Davenport wanted to keep it in Iowa, the Illinois jurisdictions worked together to get the airport on that side of the Mississippi. That is the *only* instance which any of the Quad-City officials could list in which there was any conflict between alliances of Quad-City jurisdictions pitted against each other. Not only are alliances not the normal situation in the Quad-City area, they hardly exist at all in recent Quad-City history, insofar as any of these officials can recall.

There is another type of interjurisdictional conflict which may also be vitally important for the future of a metropolitan area. This concerns goals for the jurisdictions and the area. This type of conflict is probably less likely to surface in the press, even if it occurs. All Quad-City officials were asked to list their own major goals as public officials. The goals listed by the officials will not be analyzed here, but following this question the respondents were asked three follow-up questions:

Do you think that these goals are in conflict with the goals of any of these other local Quad-City area governments?

Will you need any active assistance or cooperation from people in any of these other Quad-City local governments to achieve your own or your department's goals?

(If yes), do you think you will actually be able to get the active assistance or cooperation from these people in the other Quad-City area local governments that you think you will need?

Of the 227 respondents, 200 were able to list at least one goal they had for their city. One hundred and eighty-nine, or 95.0 per cent, of these officials did not feel their goals were in conflict with the goals of any of the other jurisdictions. No more than two respondents from any one of the jurisdictions indicated their goals were in conflict with other Quad-City goals. The elected officials were slightly more prone to see a conflict in goals than were the other officials, but even with the mayors and councilmen less than 10 per cent perceived that any of their plans conflicted with the plans of other Quad-City jurisdictions. Sixty-four of these 200 officials, or 32 per cent, indicated that they would need some assistance from another jurisdiction to achieve their goals. Large city officials indicated a need for outside assistance more frequently than small jurisdiction officials (50/134, or 37.3 per cent of the large city officials, and 14/66, or 22.2 per cent of the small jurisdiction officials). Sixty of the 64 officials who thought they would need assistance were willing to estimate whether they would actually be able to get the help they needed from other jurisdictions. Only four did not think they would get the assistance they needed. The Quad-City officials overwhelmingly believe their own goals are not in conflict with what the other jurisdictions are planning. If their programs have deleterious effects on neighboring jurisdictions, it is not apparent to these officials. To the extent that their own goals require assistance from other jurisdictions, these officials are optimistic that they will get the needed help.

The respondents were also asked what they thought should be the major goals for the Quad-City area as a whole. Once again no analysis of their responses to this question is included in this study. They were then asked "Do you think that the people in these other Quad-City area local governments would generally agree with your assessment of goals?" Of 152 officials who were able to list at least one goal for the Quad-City area as a whole, only 12, or 8.0 per cent, thought there would be any general disagreement with their goals. The public officials do not see that their goals are in conflict with other jurisdictions. Their interpretations are that the interjurisdictional political environment in which they operate is permissive and even helpful in implementing goals and plans.

Despite the emphasis of students of metropolitan affairs upon interjurisdictional conflict, this does not seem to be a very serious problem in the Quad-City area. Few overt conflicts occur. Those that do arise have little spillover impact upon other dealings between these same jurisdictions. They do not seem to leave a legacy of bitterness or unhappiness between the jurisdictions. These generalizations must be termed tentative, of course, due to the few instances of conflict which were found. Goals for the individual jurisdictions and the Quad-City area as a whole are seen by the officials as widely acceptable to their neighboring jurisdictions. The major perception of these public officials is of interjurisdictional cooperation, not conflict.

8

Stability in the Quad-City
Metropolitan Political Community

The central concern of this book has been to explain how a metropolitan political community composed of many formally autonomous local governments maintains itself. The study has attempted to explore as many potential processes of political integration as possible. From the data analysis of transactions in the preceding chapters, it is possible to draw some conclusions about the maintenance of the pluralistic Quad-City metropolitan system. The system is maintained through a variety of extensively used networks of exchange among the jurisdictional subsystems. These separate networks of direct and indirect exchange are used frequently and recurringly. The categorization of interjurisdictional exchanges as being ad hoc or sporadic within metropolitan areas is not accurate for the Quad-City area, for many different processes of direct exchange are regularly used among these separate jurisdictions.

PROCESSES OF INTEGRATION

Interjurisdictional agreements are frequent within the area, and they deal with a wide variety of subjects. These agreements, in dealing with many major issues of urban life, provide for a much more significant amount of cooperative effort within the metropolitan political community than could be anticipated from studies made within other metropolitan areas.

Most Quad-City officials have contact with officials in other area jurisdictions in the course of their official duties. These exchanges are frequent and systematic, and they deal with issues which are related and which recur over time. Since they cannot be characterized as ad hoc events, this easy system of interpersonal exchange is an important process of integration in the area. The integrative role of the professional and municipal associations to which many of the Quad-City officials belong is also very important, for under the auspices of these associations many exchanges occur. Social organizations are another means by which the area officials come in contact with one another. Almost half of the officials report meeting in this manner —and many have frequent contact in this process of political integration. Political party activity involves more than one fourth of the respondents in joint activity. This is the least of all the processes of direct exchange analyzed in the study, but it is still a substantial mechanism. In addition, Quad-City officials frequently have business associations with officials from other jurisdictions, and many also have personal friendships. All of these processes of direct exchange contribute to the political integration of activities within the metropolitan area. The cumulative evidence from the analysis of these separate measures of direct communication is of a highly-developed metropolitan political structure, with overlapping patterns of recurring exchanges among the elected and appointed public officials.

In addition to direct processes of political integration, the Quad-City plural political community is maintained through indirect processes of integration. Personally involved and influential individuals, interest groups, and the major corporate interests have been found to be active throughout the area, but particularly in the larger cities. By their activities they contribute to the creation and maintenance of a single metropolitan political system. The Quad-City political community is partially maintained because the same sets of individuals, interest groups and major corporate interests are involved in the political life of many of the jurisdictional subsystems. As noted earlier, a key element in the creation of a stable pluralistic security community is the development of a community-wide leadership structure, not bound by the jurisdictional walls. It is also a frequent lament that metropolitan wide leadership does not exist and probably cannot exist so long as separate jurisdictions divide metropolitan areas. The evidence developed from this study of active and influential individuals, interest groups, and major corporate interests, is that a metropolitan-wide leadership structure can and does exist within the Quad-City area. Newsmen covering municipal affairs have been found to be of some importance as intermediaries between the separate jurisdictions. Their activity also accounts for some indirect integration of political action. Even the municipal consultants who operate in the metropolitan area may account for some metropolitan integration. Thus, the Quad-City plural community is maintained because of indirect processes of integration as well as through the direct exchanges among the jurisdictions, and is a well-developed metropolitan political structure.

The Mississippi River state border proves to be a substantial barrier to direct exchanges among the jurisdictions. It has a measurable impact on all of the processes of direct exchange, yet what may be more notable is the extensiveness of the exchanges which do occur across the border. The only process of direct exchange which does not transcend the state border in very large measure is contact through the political parties.

The direct contacts between contiguous jurisdictions are considerably more extensive than contacts between noncontiguous jurisdictions. But exchanges among noncontiguous jurisdictions are common. A special set of relationships—"satellite-sun" combinations—has been found to exist between large jurisdictions and immediately adjacent small municipalities. The more extensive exchanges among intrastate partners, as compared to interstate ones, and contiguous municipalities over noncontiguous ones may reflect nothing more than that many more issues of interjurisdictional concern arise among the municipalities on the same side of the Mississippi River, and between contiguous jurisdictions. The lessened but still extensive interstate and noncontiguous contact may not represent much of a barrier to communication. It may partly represent the occurrence of fewer spillover problems.

The five large cities of Davenport, Rock Island, Moline, East Moline, and Bettendorf have very extensive dealings with one another. The five small jurisdictions in the Quad-City area have comparatively few contacts among themselves. These smaller municipalities, individually, have consistently more contact with larger cities than with the other small jurisdictions—a finding worth reflection.

As time-space constraints become less imperative, large jurisdictions are coming to have more political and service problems with consequences in other large cities. This megalopolitan development is already upon us. The Quad-City study suggests that it will be possible for separate large cities to have extensive integration of activities among themselves without formal unification. The ability of the five large Quad-City jurisdictions to coordinate activities is some evidence that a megalopolitan politics of bargaining may be adequate for the maintenance of a political system.

The consistently low level of exchanges among the five small jurisdictions clearly raises some serious questions about interpretations of metropolitan politics based upon a purported alliance of small suburban jurisdictions against central cities. Consistent "alliances" of any kind are almost unheard of in the Quad-Cities. The small jurisdictions have considerably more contact with the large cities than they do with other small jurisdictions. Significant parts of the big city–small jurisdiction dealing are non quid pro quo arrangements. The small jurisdictions are more dependent upon and preoccupied with the large jurisdictions than is reciprocated. This also makes the possibility of alliances among the small jurisdictions against the large ones seem quite unlikely.

PARTICIPANTS IN DIRECT EXCHANGES

The involvement of the mayors and councilmen in the intergovernmental activity within the Quad-City area is surprisingly extensive. Probably because a large part of prior research on local intergovernmental relations has concentrated on administrative relations, the involvement of these elected political leaders seems particularly impressive. As measured by activity, these elected officers are not localist vis-à-vis the orientation of the administrators. They are crucially and extensively involved in the metropolitan exchanges.

The direct exchanges among the public officials with functionally equivalent positions in the separate jurisdictions was high, as could reasonably be expected on the basis of other research on intergovernmental relations. But the extensive dealings among officials who were not functional equivalents was startling, and probably important. While intergovernmental relations in general may be promoting functionally autonomous political organization, a recurring hypothesis, this is far from the only channel of contact among the local officials. The extensive interjurisdictional contact among nonfunctionally equivalent officials in the Quad-Cities is probably the result of relatively low differentiation and specialization within these municipal bureaucracies. The lack of differentiation was particularly apparent among the smaller jurisdictions, but was notable in some of the large cities also.

MUTUAL ADJUSTMENT, SPECIALIZATION, AND COMPETITION

"Mutual adjustment" as a conscious process of integration is not extensive in the Quad-City political community. The public officials rarely acknowledge making calculations about complementing, rather than duplicating, services already available through the activities and programs of other jurisdictions. Perhaps these officials believe that specialization itself is not entirely proper, because a municipality should provide its citizens with all the local government services they need. The extent of unconscious "mutual adjustment," and its importance for integrating political activity was not measured in the survey. On the other hand, the respondents freely acknowledge that frequently they rely upon the experiences and examples of the other cities when considering their own programs.

The Quad-City officials are found to be in some self-conscious competition with each other on some matters where the competition may actually improve the quality of public services throughout the area. There is widely reported conscious competition over levels of service provided citizens. Conscious competition over budget levels and tax rates is less evident, but far from uncommon. Salary comparisons and competition, particularly among the large jurisdictions, is extensive. In all of these situations, the competition may lead to more effective use of resources, and may keep the individual municipal service levels in comparable and proportionate relation.

INTERJURISDICTIONAL CONFLICT

The Quad-City municipalities do not have many interjurisdictional conflicts, and those which occur seem to involve few measurable deleterious spillover consequences. The legacy of political conflict does not seem to lead to any break in the diplomatic relations between the jurisdictions. The survey respondents overwhelmingly perceive of the intergovernmental environment as one of cooperation, not conflict, in spite of the preponderant emphasis on conflict in the published case analyses of metropolitan politics.

CONCLUSION

The Quad-City political system is stable and well-integrated, and no jurisdictions are isolated. Once its processes of integration are measured, there is no longer a mystery as to how the system is able to maintain itself. Although this metropolitan structure is complicated and extensive, it does work.

While the Quad-City system is able to operate at a level satisfactory to enough Quad-City residents so that it is stable and predictable, this should not be construed as very compelling evidence for the retention of this particular system over, say, a formally unified or federated metropolitan government. The evidence from this study should provide a warning to social engineers that the present political system in metropolitan areas is probably well-entrenched, and operating more rationally and effectively than many will acknowledge. Formal unification of the metropolitan area would not result in instituting order in place of chaos. It would replace one form of order with another.

The successful operation of the Quad-City political system measured in terms of survival is not the only basis for judgment about the merits of reform proposals, although it is one legitimate criterion. Some of the important issues of metropolitan organization which are not "answered" by these measurements of processes of political integration are the difficulties encountered by the creation of class barriers between jurisdictions, tax equity and redistribution questions, and even the classic and hoary issue of "efficiency in government."

Perhaps the impact of metropolitan political organization upon racial relations is the major critical question of public policy which deserves, probably demands attention. The immanent control of some central cities by black political leaders raises anew the question of metropolitan reorganization. It is by no means clear, for example, whether black control of central city jurisdictions will enhance Negro life choices in such cities, or do the reverse. Will Negro-controlled municipalities be able to cooperate and integrate political activities with white-controlled suburban jurisdictions? Will white-dominated legislatures be as responsive to municipal problems of Negro-controlled cities as they would be to white-controlled metropolitan-wide jurisdictions where Negro minorities engage in coalition politics? With the lack of fiscal capacity of many municipal governments, it is even possible that the dependence on outside financial help may result in the instituting of a federal system for Negro-controlled cities which approaches (or exceeds) colonial practices of indirect rule. But it is hardly clear what will occur, or what are the options.

In spite of the extensive attention paid to metropolitan political organization over the years, the subject continues to raise profound questions of public policy and unresolved but vital research possibilities for political scientists. This book has been largely an exercise in political mapping. It describes political structure. The study may be taken as a first essential step in exploring major political questions about metropolitan areas, for the research does not cover such central issues of the discipline as who rules and who benefits under this or alternate forms of political organization of metropolitan areas. What this book has done is uncover the ways in which a metropolitan political system composed of many separate jurisdictions is able to be maintained.

Appendix A

Technical Appendix

INTERVIEW SCHEDULE

The interview schedule developed for the Quad-City survey used as a model the interview schedule from the Siouxland Study.[1] A few of the questions were almost unchanged. The interview schedule is essentially a close-ended, multiple-option instrument, and was pretested on volunteer public officials in the Quad-Cities. To the extent the instrument was changed, these volunteers were subsequently reinterviewed. The questions were slightly different between the elected officials and the appointed ones. Two separate but very similar interview instruments were used, which seemed to cause no difficulty.

In the earlier Siouxland Study respondents were asked to choose the best of a series of options about frequency of various occurrences beginning with "once a week or more," "less than once a week, but at least once a month," etc. This caused some respondent dismay, especially on occasions where a respondent had frequent contact over a short space of time (i.e., many exchanges during the month of August, but none through the rest of the year). In the Quad-City instrument these questions were reworked to ask frequency within the last year. This seemed to work satisfactorily. It also seemed to be a more precise indicator of frequency than that used by Weidner in his important study of Minnesota officials ("Never," "Rarely," "Occasionally," "Often," "Very Often").[2] While the reliability of respon-

1. H. Paul Friesema, Communications, Coordination, and Control Among Local Governments in the Siouxland: A Study of Intergovernmental Relations (Iowa City: Institute of Public Affairs, University of Iowa, 1965), Appendix A..
2. Edward W. Weidner, Intergovernmental Relations as Seen by Public Officials (Minneapolis: University of Minnesota Press, 1960), Appendix 1.

dent estimates is a serious problem, at least the respondents and the researchers have the same referent in the estimates.

There is a serious problem in relying upon estimates of respondents as to their contact with others.[3] There seemed to be no other practical way to measure this many interactions and respondents directly. These estimates, for all their potential distortion, remained the only practical recourse. In all probability the public officials understate, to some unmeasurable degree, the amount of their actual contact and the frequency with which it occurs. There seems to be little reason for these public officials to "remember" events that did not occur, but much reason for them to forget other events which did occur. One innovation which may be possible in the future for improving upon this difficulty might be to adapt the procedure developed by Caplow, Stryker, and Wallace in *The Urban Ambience*.[4] In that study of barrio interaction in Puerto Rico, the researchers matched up each two possible interacting individuals as to their estimates of frequency. The lowest common denomination of agreement was coded as the measure of interaction. That could not be done in the Quad-City estimate, for all exchanges were not necessarily with officials in other jurisdictions who were also respondents. Public officials from one jurisdiction frequently had contact with officials in other jurisdictions who were not department heads or elected officials. Nonetheless, in similar studies it may be possible to get a more reliable indicator of interaction by adopting some variant of the procedure used in *The Urban Ambience*.

SURVEY

The interview schedule was administered to the public officials who were the respondents over approximately a six-month period, beginning in the summer of 1966. Most interviews were conducted by three interviewers: the author and two other staff members of the Institute of Public Affairs at The University of Iowa. The interviews were conducted in a variety of settings, including the respondents' governmental offices, private offices, homes, and even cars. The interviews were held from fairly early in the morning to quite late at night. This flexibility was thought necessary in order to achieve a 100 per cent population survey. Other interviewers were

3. See the discussion in Benjamin Walter, *Bureaucratic Communication: A Statistical Analysis of Influence* (Chapel Hill: Institute for Research-Social Science, University of North Carolina, 1963), VI.
4. Theodore Caplow, Sheldon Stryker, and Samuel E. Wallace, *The Urban Ambience* (Totowa, N.J.: Bedminster Press, 1964).

also used upon occasion. This occurred with some of the municipal elected officials. For a number of the jurisdictions, the mayors set up appointments with councilmen either directly following a council meeting or even during an extended break in the middle of a council meeting. These were evening meetings, so it was possible to recruit other Institute staff members to assist in this interviewing. All interviewers were experienced in this work, with the exception of one of the regular interviewers, who was trained by the other two.

The interviews lasted anywhere from fifteen minutes to over two hours. The interview schedule was difficult to administer, requiring frequent back-paging to check one answer in order to determine what to ask next, but did not prove difficult to answer. Usually the questions piqued the respondents' interest and it became a problem to close out the interview. Whenever the respondents were faced with difficult options, cards were presented to them with the choices. There were few overt signs of respondent fatigue, with the one notable exception of the sequence of questions on *municipal activists* (Chapter 5). By the fifth go-round on that sequence of questions, many respondents were bored. For this reason, the analysis lumps the responses at the four and five level into a single group.

The survey was administered to all of the elected officials from the ten jurisdictions, and all those other officials who were defined as department heads, or heads of independent boards and commissions. The definition of the population was extremely difficult for none of the ten jurisdictions had anything like an organization chart adequate to our purpose.[5] Even in the large cities, organization is less than fully articulated. The interviewers' probing to establish who was responsible to whom, and who reported directly to the mayor, etc., sometimes resulted in answers that were vague in the extreme.

The most difficult decisions in this regard concerned independent boards and commissions. Some "on the books" did not actually operate. Some involved only ex officio members. Some were not independent of a department whose executive officer was interviewed. In all these events, the head of that board or commission, so-called, was not interviewed. Whenever a board or commission had a full-time executive officer, whatever his title (even if he was not "full-time" with the board or commission, but was with the jurisdiction) he was the chosen respondent. When there was no such official, the "chairman," "president," or whoever headed the appointed board was the respondent.

While there were problems in selecting the "population," the problems

5. Davenport had an excellent one, but out of date. Harry Smith and Frederick Suder-mann, *A Survey of Municipal Organization and Administration—Davenport, Iowa* (Iowa City: Institute of Public Affairs, University of Iowa, 1961).

of completing a total population survey were not as great as anticipated. There were no interview refusals. The incidents of refusal to answer any specific question were also extremely low. This occurred despite the mildly threatening or embarrassing nature of a few questions (i.e., relating dealings with influential people, or asking civil servants about their political party activities).

STATISTICS

No statistical tests of significance are presented in this study—for two sufficient reasons. First, the survey is largely exploratory. Very few specific hypotheses are stated. Consequently statistical tests of significance are inappropriate. Second, the survey is of the total defined population of Quad-City elected and appointed officials. It is not a random sample. Thus, the relationships which have been found are the real ones for this particular population at this time. While tests of significance are frequently found in population surveys, what they indicate is problematical. They are surely "suggestive," but they may, in this instance at least, suggest too much. They may suggest to the casual reader that the Quad-Cities are the "sample," and that the test of significance is for cities within metropolitan areas. But the ten jurisdictions within the Quad-Cities are not randomly selected cases of individual jurisdictions within metropolitan areas. The danger of presenting statistical tests of significance in this study outweigh the marginal usefulness of that exercise. For a full discussion of the rationale for this decision to avoid statistical tests, it may be useful to cite the methodological appendices of Lipset's Union Democracy[6] and the Wahlke, Eulau et al., book The Legislative System.[7]

DATA MANIPULATION

The responses were coded by the author and check coded by other Institute staff members. The author made all questionable coding decisions. In all, six decks of information were coded for each respondent. The responses

6. Seymour Martin Lipset, Martin A. Trow, and James S. Coleman, Union Democracy: The Internal Politics of the International Typographical Union (New York: Free Press of Glencoe, 1956), Appendix I.
7. John C. Wahlke et al., The Legislative System (New York: John Wiley & Sons, 1962), Appendices.

to a few parts of the survey were grouped by *jurisdiction* rather than by *individual*. They were coded separately, and analyzed with only the aid of a desk calculator. The principal items analyzed in this manner were inter-jurisdictional agreements (Chapter 3) and the role of municipal consultants (Chapter 6).

The other data was run through the 7044 computer of The University of Iowa Computer Center, using a NUCROS program of cross classification of variables.[8]

8. For a discussion of the NUCROS program see Kenneth Janda, *Data Processing: Applications to Political Research* (Evanston: Northwestern University Press, 1965), particularly Appendix C-1.

Appendix B

Subject Code—Interjurisdictional Agreements

		Number of Agreements
1.	Mutual Aid—fire	18
2.	Mutual Aid—police	21
3.	Mutual Aid—civil defense	5
4.	Mutual Aid—civil rights	7
5.	Mutual Aid (back-up)—sewers	3
6.	Mutual Aid (back-up)—water	4
7.	Metropolitan planning	15
8.	Metropolitan airport	3
9.	Milk inspection agreement	3
10.	Police radio tie-in	23
11.	Arrest information system	12
12.	Coordinated road block system	14
13.	Personnel and program coordinated park agreement	6
14.	Interlibrary loans	15
15.	Film co-op (library)	15
16.	River Bend library system	8
17.	Unified plumbing code	10
18.	Unified building code system	21
19.	Food inspection reciprocity	5
20.	Health notification	7
21.	Equipment maintenance—parts exchange	3
22.	Policing agreement on R. I. bridge	1
23.	Joint planning jurisdiction agreement	2
24.	City planning reciprocity	3
25.	Sewer line use agreement	3
26.	Baseball and softball coordinated program	2
27.	Alternate year service—border roads	3
28.	Coordinated snow removal	3

	Number of Agreements
29. Water pollution control agreement (sewage disposal)	2
30. Library reference materials exchange	4
31. Annexation agreement on sewage disposal use	1
32. Border traffic lights agreement	1
33. Civil Defense service agreement	1
34. Street engineering	1
35. Milk inspection service	3
36. Swimming pool use agreement	1
37. Land fill and refuse use agreement	2
38. Sale of water	1

Bibliography

Bibliography

BOOKS

Adrian, Charles R. *Public Attitudes and Metropolitan Decision-Making*. Eighth Annual Wheritt Lecture on Local Government. Pittsburgh: University of Pittsburgh, 1962.

Agger, Robert E.; Goldrich, Daniel; and Swanson, Bert E. *The Rulers and the Ruled: Political Power and Impotence in American Communities*. New York: John Wiley & Sons, 1964.

Alternative Approaches to Governmental Reorganization in Metropolitan Areas. Washington, D.C.: Advisory Commission on Intergovernmental Relations Information Report, 1962.

Anderson, William. *Intergovernmental Relations in Review*. Minneapolis: University of Minnesota Press, 1960.

Armstrong, Perry A. *The Sauks and the Black Hawk War*. Springfield, Ill.: H. W. Rokkar, Printer and Binder, 1887.

Banfield, Edward, and Grodzins, Morton. *Government and Housing in Metropolitan Areas*. New York: McGraw-Hill, 1958.

Banfield, Edward. *Political Influence*. New York: Free Press of Glencoe, 1961.

Bateman, Newton, and Selby, Paul, eds. *Historical Encyclopedia of Illinois and History of Rock Island County*. Chicago: Munsell Publishing Co., 1914.

Black Hawk, An Autobiography. Edited by Donald Jackson. Urbana: University of Illinois Press, 1964.

Bollens, John C., ed. *Exploring the Metropolitan Community*. Berkeley and Los Angeles: University of California Press, 1961.

Bollens, John C., and Schmandt, Henry. *The Metropolis: Its People, Politics and Economic Life*. New York: Harper & Row, 1965.

Booth, David A. *Metropolitics: The Nashville Consolidation*. East Lansing: Institute for Community Development and Service, Michigan State University, 1963.

Burrows, J. M. D. *Fifty Years in Iowa*. Davenport: Glass and Co., Printers and Binders, 1888. Reprinted in *The Early Days of Rock Island and Davenport*. Chicago: Lakeside Press, 1942.

Caplow, Theodore; Stryker, Sheldon; and Wallace, Samuel E. *The Urban Ambience*. Totowa, N.J.: Bedminster Press, 1964.

Community Leadership and Decision-Making. Iowa City: Institute of Public Affairs, University of Iowa, 1967.

Crouch, Winston. *Intergovernmental Relations*. Metropolitan Los Angeles Study, vol. 15. Los Angeles: Haynes Foundation, 1954.

Crouch, Winston, and Dinerman, Beatrice. *Southern California Metropolis:*

A Study in Development of Government for a Metropolitan Area. Berkeley and Los Angeles: University of California Press, 1964.

Danielson, Michael N. *Federal-Metropolitan Politics and the Commuter Crisis.* New York: Columbia University Press, 1965.

D'Antonio, William, and Form, William H. *Influentials in Two Border Cities: A Study in Community Decision-Making.* South Bend: University of Notre Dame Press, 1965.

Deutsch, Karl W. *Nationalism and Social Communication: An Inquiry into the Foundations of Nationalism.* Cambridge, Mass.: M.I.T. Press, 1953.

————. *The Nerves of Government: Models of Political Communication and Control.* New York: Free Press of Glencoe, 1963.

Deutsch, Karl W. *Political Community at the International Level.* Garden City, N.Y.: Doubleday & Co., 1954.

Deutsch, Karl W. et al. *Political Community and the North Atlantic Area.* Princeton: Princeton University Press, 1957.

Easton, David. *A Framework for Political Analysis.* Englewood Cliffs, N.J.: Prentice-Hall, 1965.

Emerging Problems in Housing and Urban Redevelopment. Iowa City: Institute of Public Affairs, University of Iowa, 1965.

Espenshade, Edward P., Jr. "Urban Development at the Upper Rapids of the Mississippi River." Ph.D. dissertation, Department of Geography, University of Chicago, 1944.

Factors Affecting Voter Reactions to Governmental Reorganizations in Metropolitan Areas. Washington, D.C.: Advisory Commission on Intergovernmental Relations Information Report, May 1962.

Feasibility of the Unification of City Governments of Rock Island, Moline and East Moline. Chicago: J. L. Jacobs Co., August 1965.

Feasibility of the Unification of City Governments of Rock Island, Moline and East Moline: Supplementary Report. Chicago: J. L. Jacobs Co., October 1965.

Fetzer, John Clark. *A Study in City Building: Davenport, Iowa.* Davenport: Davenport Chamber of Commerce, 1945.

Friesema, H. Paul. *Communications, Coordination, and Control Among Local Governments in the Siouxland: A Study of Intergovernmental Relations.* Iowa City: Institute of Public Affairs, University of Iowa, 1965.

Gottman, Jean. *Megalopolis.* New York: Twentieth Century Fund, 1961.

Gove, Samuel K. *The Lakewood Plan.* Urbana: Institute of Government and Public Affairs, University of Illinois, 1961.

Governmental Affairs Foundation. *Metropolitan Surveys: A Digest.* Chicago: Public Administration Service, 1958.

Graves, W. Brooke. *American Intergovernmental Relations.* New York: Charles Scribner's Sons, 1964.

Greer, Scott. *The Emerging City: Myth and Reality.* New York: Free Press of Glencoe, 1962.

————. *Governing the Metropolis.* New York: John Wiley & Sons, 1962.

————. *Metropolitics: A Study of Political Culture.* New York: John Wiley & Sons, 1963.

Grodzins, Morton. *The American System.* Edited by Daniel J. Elazar. Chicago: Rand, McNally & Co., 1966.

Guetzkow, Harold. *Multiple Loyalties: Theoretical Approach to a Problem in*

International Organization. Princeton: Princeton University Press, 1955.

Hauser, Philip M., and Schnore, Leo F., eds. *The Study of Urbanization.* New York: John Wiley & Sons, 1965.

Havard, William C., and Corty, Floyd L. *Rural-Urban Consolidation: The Merger of Governments in the Baton Rouge Area.* Baton Rouge: Louisiana State University Press, 1965.

Hawkins, Brett W. *Nashville Metro: The Politics of City-County Consolidation.* Nashville: Vanderbilt University Press, 1966.

Hays, Forbes B. *Community Leadership.* New York and London: Columbia University Press, 1965.

Holden, Matthew, Jr. *Intergovernmental Agreements in the Cleveland Metropolitan Area.* Staff Report to Study Group on Governmental Organization, Cleveland Metropolitan Service Commission, 1958.

Hoover, Edgar M., and Vernon, Raymond. *Anatomy of a Metropolis.* Garden City, N.J.: Doubleday & Co., 1962.

Hunter, Floyd. *Community Power Structure: A Study of Decision Makers.* Chapel Hill: University of North Carolina Press, 1953.

Jacob, Philip E., and Toscano, James V., eds. *The Integration of Political Communities.* Philadelphia and New York: J. B. Lippincott, 1964.

Janda, Kenneth. *Data Processing: Applications to Political Research.* Evanston: Northwestern University Press, 1965.

Janowitz, Morris, ed. *Community Political Systems.* New York: Free Press of Glencoe, 1961.

Jennings, M. Kent. *Community Influentials: The Elites of Atlanta.* New York: Free Press of Glencoe, 1964.

Jones, Victor. *Metropolitan Government.* Chicago: University of Chicago Press, 1942.

Lazarsfeld, Paul F., and Rosenberg, Morris, eds. *The Language of Social Research.* New York: Free Press of Glencoe, 1965.

Lindblom, Charles E. *The Intelligence of Democracy: Decision-Making Through Mutual Adjustment.* New York: Free Press of Glencoe, 1965.

Lipset, Seymour Martin; Trow, Martin A.; and Coleman, James S. *Union Democracy: The Internal Politics of the International Typographical Union.* New York: Free Press of Glencoe, 1956.

Lynch, Kevin. *The Image of the City.* Cambridge, Mass.: M.I.T. Press, 1960.

Lynch, Myra. *Illinois Local Government,* 2nd ed. Urbana: Institute of Government and Public Affairs, University of Illinois, 1965.

Maass, Arthur, ed. *Area and Power.* New York: Free Press of Glencoe, 1959.

———. *Muddy Waters.* Cambridge: Harvard University Press, 1951.

Mandelbaum, Seymour J. *Boss Tweed's New York.* New York: John Wiley & Sons, 1965.

Martin, Roscoe C. et al. *Decisions in Syracuse.* Bloomington: Indiana University Press, 1961.

Martin, Roscoe C., and Price, Douglas. *The Metropolis and Its Problems.* Syracuse: Syracuse University Seminar on Metropolitan Research, 1959.

Martin, Roscoe C. *Metropolis in Transition: Local Adaptation to Changing Needs.* Washington, D.C.: Housing and Home Finance Agency, 1963.

Mather, George B. *A Citizen's Guide to Iowa Municipal Government and Elections.* Iowa City: Institute of Public Affairs, University of Iowa, 1959.

Meier, Richard L. *A Communications Theory of Urban Growth.* Cambridge,

Mass.: M.I.T. Press, 1962.

————. *Megalopolis Formation in the Midwest.* Ann Arbor: School of Natural Resources, University of Michigan, 1965.

Merritt, Richard L. *Symbols of American Community, 1735–1775.* New Haven: Yale University Press, 1966.

Metropolitan Area Unification in the Battle Creek Urban Area. Detroit: Citizens' Research Council of Michigan, 1966.

Modernizing Local Government. New York: Committee for Economic Development, 1966.

Mowitz, Robert, and Wright, Deil S. *Profile of a Metropolis.* Detroit: Wayne State University Press, 1962.

Polsby, Nelson W. *Community Power and Political Theory.* New Haven: Yale University Press, 1963.

Presthus, Robert. *Men at the Top: A Study of Community Power.* New York: Oxford University Press, 1964.

Proceedings of the 1964 Urban Policy Conference. Iowa City: Institute of Public Affairs, University of Iowa, 1964.

A Prospectus on the Quad-City Area. Rock Island: Iowa-Illinois Industrial Development Group, n.d.

Russett, Bruce M. *Community and Contention: Britain and America in the Twentieth Century.* Cambridge, Mass.: M.I.T. Press, 1963.

Sayre, Wallace, and Kaufman, Herbert. *Governing New York City: Politics in the Metropolis.* New York: Russell Sage Foundation, 1961.

Schmandt, Henry, and Standing, William H. *The Milwaukee Metropolitan Study Commission.* Bloomington: Indiana University Press, 1965.

Shannon, Claude E., and Weaver, Warren. *The Mathematical Theory of Communication.* Urbana: University of Illinois Press, 1949.

Sjoberg, Gideon. *The Preindustrial City.* New York: Free Press of Glencoe, 1960.

Smallwood, Frank. *Greater London: The Politics of Metropolitan Reform.* Indianapolis: Bobbs-Merrill Co., 1965.

Smith, Harry, and Sudermann, Frederick. *A Survey of Municipal Organization and Administration—Davenport, Iowa.* Iowa City: Institute of Public Affairs, University of Iowa, 1961.

Spencer, J. W. *Reminiscences of Pioneer Life in the Mississippi Valley.* Davenport: Griggs, Watson and Day, 1872. Republished in *The Early Days of Rock Island and Davenport.* Chicago: Lakeside Press, 1942.

Sofen, Edward. *The Miami Metropolitan Experiment.* Bloomington: Indiana University Press, 1963.

Studenski, Paul. *Government of Metropolitan Areas.* New York: National Municipal League, 1930.

Wade, Richard C. *The Urban Frontier.* Chicago and London: University of Chicago Press, 1959.

Wahlke, John et al. *The Legislative System.* New York: John Wiley & Sons, 1962.

Warren, Robert O., *Government in Metropolitan Regions: A Reappraisal of Fractionated Political Organization.* Davis: Institute of Governmental Affairs, University of California, 1966.

Weidner, Edward W. *Intergovernmental Relations as Seen by Public Officials.* Minneapolis: University of Minnesota Press, 1960.

Winters, John M. *Interstate Metropolitan Areas.* Ann Arbor: University of Michigan Legal Publications, 1962.

Wood, Robert C. *1400 Governments.* Garden City, N.J.: Doubleday & Co., Anchor Books, 1961.

_____. *Suburbia: Its People and Their Politics.* Boston: Houghton-Mifflin Co., 1958.

ARTICLES AND PAPERS

Adrian, Charles R. "Metropology: Folklore and Field Research." *Public Administration Review* 21 (Summer 1961), 148–157.

"Business and Government: Planning in the Quad-Cities." *New York Times,* February 27, 1967, 43.

Bylinski, Gene. "Farm Technology Plows Ahead at Deere." *Fortune,* December 1966, 147–151, 278–280.

Carrell, Jeptha J. "Learning to Work Together." *National Municipal Review* 43 (November 1954), 526–533.

Coke, James G. "The Lesser Metropolitan Areas of Illinois." *Illinois Government* 15. Urbana: Institute of Government and Public Affairs, University of Illinois, November 1962.

Crouch, Winston. "Conflict and Cooperation Among Local Governments in the Metropolis." *Annals* of the American Academy of Political and Social Science 359 (May 1965), 60–70.

Deutsch, Karl W. "Transaction Flows as Indicators of Political Cohesion." In *The Integration of Political Communities,* editors Philip Jacob, and James V. Toscano, pp. 75–97. Philadelphia and New York: J. B. Lippincott, 1964.

Dye, Thomas R. et al. "Differentiation and Cooperation in a Metropolitan Area." *Midwest Journal of Political Science* 7 (May 1963), 145–155.

Dye, Thomas R. "Metropolitan Integration by Bargaining Among Sub-Areas." *American Behavioral Scientist* 5 (May 1962), 5.

Friesema, H. Paul. "The Metropolis and the Maze of Local Government." *Urban Affairs Quarterly* 2 (December 1966), 68–90.

_____. "Some Organizational Implications of Intergovernmental Activity within Metropolitan Areas." *Midwest Review of Public Administration* 1 (February 1967), 11–16.

Gould, James M. "Pioneer Life." In *Historical Encyclopedia of Illinois and History of Rock Island County,* editors Bateman, Newton, and Selby, pp. 646–647. Chicago: Munsell Publishing Co., 1914.

Gove, Samuel K. "Local Government and Local Politics." In *Illinois Local Government,* 2nd ed., edited by Myra Lynch, pp. 28–40. Urbana: Institute of Government and Public Affairs, University of Illinois, 1965.

Gove, Samuel K., and Silverstein, Louis. "Political Representation and Interstate Urban Agencies," *Illinois Government* 17. Urbana: Institute of Government and Public Affairs, June 1963.

Grant, Daniel R. "The Government of Interstate Metropolitan Areas." *Western Political Quarterly* 8 (March, 1955), 90–107.

Greer, Scott. "Dilemmas of Action Research on the Metropolitan Problem."

In *Community Political Systems,* edited by Morris Janowitz, pp. 185–206. New York: Free Press of Glencoe, 1961.

Hawley, Amos H., and Zimmer, Basil G. "Resistance to Unification in a Metropolitan Community." In *Community Political Systems,* edited by Morris Janowitz, pp. 146–184. New York: Free Press of Glencoe, 1961.

Herson, Lawrence J. R. "The Lost World of Municipal Government." *American Political Science Review* 51 (June 1957), 330–345.

Holden, Matthew, Jr. "The Governance of the Metropolis as a Problem in Diplomacy." *Journal of Politics* 26 (August 1964), 627–647.

Huntoon, John G. "Street Railroad and Transportation." In *Historical Encyclopedia of Illinois and History of Rock Island County,* editors Bateman, Newton, and Selby, pp. 774–779. Chicago: Munsell Publishing Co., 1914.

Jacob, Philip E., and Teune, Henry. "The Integrative Process: Guidelines for Analysis of the Bases of Political Community." In *The Integration of Political Communities,* editors Philip Jacob, and James V. Toscano, pp. 1–46. Philadelphia and New York: J. B. Lippincott, 1964.

Landecker, Werner S. "Types of Integration and Their Measurement." Reprinted in *The Language of Social Research,* editors Paul F. Lazarsfeld, and Morris Rosenberg, pp. 19–27. New York: Free Press of Glencoe, 1965.

Leibman, Charles S. et al. "Social Status, Tax Resources and Metropolitan Cooperation." *National Tax Journal* 16 (March 1963), 56–62.

Lieberson, Stanley, and Schwerian, Kent P. "Banking Functions as an Index of Inter-City Relations." *Journal of Regional Science* 4 (Summer 1962), 70–79.

Long, Norton. "Community Decision-Making." In *Community Leadership and Decision-Making.* Iowa City: Institute of Public Affairs, University of Iowa, 1967.

McElrath, Dennis. "Political and Social Implications of Urbanization." In *Proceedings of the 1964 Urban Policy Conference,* pp. 24–32. Iowa City: Institute of Public Affairs, University of Iowa, 1964.

Meese, William A. "Indian History." In *Historical Encyclopedia of Illinois and History of Rock Island County,* editors Bateman, Newton, and Selby, pp. 617–625. Chicago: Munsell Publishing Co., 1914.

Miller, Delbert. "Industry and Community Power Structure." *American Sociological Review* 23 (February 1958), 9–15.

"Mini-Megalopolis Rises along the Mississippi." *Business Week,* February 25, 1967, pp. 168–170.

Olmsted, Robert F. "County Organization and Government." In *Historical Encyclopedia of Illinois and History of Rock Island County,* editors Bateman, Newton, and Selby, pp. 636–645. Chicago: Munsell Publishing Co., 1914.

Ostrom, Vincent et al. "The Organization of Government in Metropolitan Areas: A Theoretical Inquiry." *American Political Science Review* 55 (December 1961), 831–842.

Pellegrin, Roland J., and Coates, Charles H. "Absentee-Owned Corporations and Community Power Structure." *American Journal of Sociology* 61 (March 1956), 413–419.

Richmond, Jo F., and Buehler, Roy E. "Interpersonal Communication: A Theoretical Formulation." *Journal of Communication* 12 (March 1962), 3–10.

"Rock Island Arsenal." In *Historical Enclyopedia of Illinois and History of*

Rock Island County, editors Bateman, Newton, and Selby, pp. 830–840. Chicago: Munsell Publishing Co., 1914.

Savage, I. Richard, and Deutsch, Karl W. "A Statistical Model of the Gross Analysis of Transaction Flows." *Econometrica* 28 (July 1960), 551–572.

Sayre, Wallace S., and Polsby, Nelson W. "American Political Science and the Study of Urbanization." In *The Study of Urbanization*, editors Philip M. Hauser, and Leo F. Schnore, pp. 115–156. New York: John Wiley & Sons, 1965.

Schmandt, Henry J. "Changing Directions." *National Civic Review* 54 (November 1965), 530–534.

———. "The Emerging Strategy." *National Civic Review* 55 (June 1966), 325–330.

———. "Toward Comparability in Metropolitan Research." Paper read at Conference on Comparative Research in Community Politics, November 16–19, 1966, at University of Georgia.

Schultze, Robert O. "The Bifurcation of Power in a Satellite City." In *Community Political Systems*, edited by Morris Janowitz, pp. 19–80. New York: Free Press of Glencoe, 1961.

Shannon, Lyle W. "Economic Absorption and Cultural Integration of the Urban Newcomer." In *Emerging Problems in Housing and Urban Redevelopment*, pp. 24–46. Iowa City: Institute of Public Affairs, University of Iowa, 1965.

Sharkansky, Ira. "Intergovernmental Relations in Brevard County, Florida: An Exploratory Study." Tallahassee: Urban Research Center, Florida State University, June 1966.

Toscano, James V. "Transaction Flow Analysis in Metropolitan Areas: Some Preliminary Explorations." In *The Integration of Political Communities*, editors Philip Jacob, and James V. Toscano, pp. 98–119. Philadelphia and New York: J. B. Lippincott, 1964.

Warren, Robert O. "Political Form and Metropolitan Reform." *Public Administration Review* 24 (September 1964), 180–187.

Wood, Robert C. "A Division of Power in Metropolitan Areas." In *Area and Power*, edited by Arthur Maass, pp. 53–69. New York: Free Press of Glencoe, 1959.

Wright, Deil S. "Intergovernmental Relations and Environmental Change: What Role for the States." Paper presented at seminar on Political Dynamics of Environmental Change, March 18–20, 1965, at Indiana University.

Unpublished Material

Agnew, Dwight L. "Beginnings of the Rock Island Lines, 1851–1870." Ph.D. dissertation, Department of History, University of Iowa, 1947.

Masotti, Louis H. "The Politics of Plural Communities: The Process of Political Integration in a Multi-Municipality High School District." Ph.D. dissertation, Department of Political Science, Northwestern University, 1964.

"What Do You Need to Know about the Possible Unification of our Cities?"

Mimeographed. Moline, Ill.: League of Women Voters, November 1965.

Wright, Deil S., and Van Bruggen, Edwin M. "Schools versus Sewers: An Empirical Test of the Tax Competition Thesis." Mimeographed. Iowa City: Institute of Public Affairs, University of Iowa, 1966.

Newspapers

Davenport Times-Democrat, 1955–1967.
Moline Dispatch, 1965–1967.
Rock Island Argus, 1965–1967.